Guiding Your
Teen TO A Faith
That Lasts

Discovery
House
PUBLISHERS

BOX 3566 · GRAND RAPIDS, MI 49501

*PUBLISHING BOOKS THAT FEED
THE SOUL WITH THE WORD OF GOD.*

Guiding Your
Teen TO A Faith
That Lasts

*A blueprint for building
a relationship with God*

Kevin Huggins
Phil Landrum

Guiding Your Teen to a Faith That Lasts
Copyright © 1994 by Kevin Huggins and Phil Landrum

Unless otherwise indicated, Scripture is taken from the
HOLY BIBLE, NEW INTERNATIONAL VERSION.
Copyright © 1973, 1978, 1984 International Bible Society.
Used by permission of Zondervan Bible Publishers.

Library of Congress Cataloging-in-Publication Data

Huggins, Kevin.
　　Guiding your teen to a faith that lasts : a blueprint for
building a relationship with God / Kevin Huggins, Phil
Landrum.
　　　　p.　cm.
　　ISBN 0–929239–10–5
　　1. Christian education of teenagers.　2. Parent and
teenager.　3. Parenting—Religious aspects—Christianity.
I. Landrum, Phil.　II. Title.
BV1485.H78　　1994
248.8'45—dc20　　　　　　　　　　　　　　　　94–29468
　　　　　　　　　　　　　　　　　　　　　　　　　　　CIP

Discovery House Publishers is affiliated with Radio Bible
Class, Grand Rapids, Michigan 49512

Discovery House books are distributed to the trade by Thomas
Nelson Publishers, Nashville, Tennessee 37214

Printed in the United States of America

94 95 96 97 98 99 / CHG / 10 9 8 7 6 5 4 3 2 1

WE DEDICATE THIS BOOK TO OUR GRANDPARENTS

To Oldham Mize and Serena Belle Landrum
Frank William and Johannah Marie Larson

The Christian faith of Serena Belle and Mize is legendary in the mountains of Kentucky. These two spiritual giants lived that faith in front of eleven teenage children. Because they exhibited a faith that lasts, Mize and Serena Belle will always be remembered by 37 grandchildren, 75 great grandchildren, and (to date) 25 great great grandchildren. Some of these children have already joined Serena Belle and Mize in eternity.

Johannah and Frank also exhibited this faith from the time they were teenagers in Nebraska. They moved to California, where their rock-hard Christian convictions during the desperate depression years will never be forgotten by the four teens they raised. Their faith has taken them to eternity leaving behind a shining example for 12 grandchildren and 18 great grandchildren.

To Lawrence Yancy and Bertha Elaine Huggins
Ophus and Vera Adele Cleaver

I'll never forget how each of my four grandparents lived out the Christian faith before my very eyes as I was growing up. Each had his or her unique way of expressing the faith and serving Christ in the good times and in the hard times.

The genuine way they lived their lives broke up the soil in my own heart and prepared it for the seeds of Christian faith that were later planted there.

I'll always be grateful for the way God used them to pass on a faith that lasts from their generation to my generation.

Contents

One

Why Are We Losing Our Kids?

There's the sound of pounding feet outside our homes these days—the sound of teenagers running away from the Christian beliefs we taught them.

Erica, a sophomore in college is one of the "runaways." She asks a question that chills any Christian parent's heart: "I've grown up in the church and I've been taught that once you're saved, you're always saved. But is there any way I can get out of my salvation?"

Why would Erica want to do that?

"In my home and at my church," Erica says, "to be a good Christian I had to be slim and prim. I've never been good at that. I've always been overweight. I've never been one of the beautiful people. I tried my best to be the kind of person God wanted me to be, but I never felt that I fit in.

"However, at the university I've met a lot of really nice non-Christians. For the first time in my life, I feel accepted. I can just be myself and still be loved!

"Recently, I started thinking about how heaven goes on forever. Frankly, I'd rather spend eternity in hell with people who accept me than eternity in heaven with a bunch of snobs."

After his junior year of high school, Jason joined a summer drama group. When he returned, he refused to go to church anymore, and his parents asked why.

Jason looked at them almost apologetically and explained, "I don't believe what those people believe—especially the youth pastor. The Sunday before I left, he spent the entire meeting talking about homosexuals and how evil they are and how they are our enemies.

"That's just not true. My best friend this summer was a homosexual. He was the most sincere, most respected guy in the group. Also the most talented. Sure, he has his problems, but he showed me more acceptance in twelve weeks than anyone in my youth group did in five years. There's a big world out there, and my church doesn't understand it."

Then Jason paused and looked down. In a quieter voice he said, "Mom . . . Dad . . . you know what bothered me most? You would have said the same thing as the youth pastor."

Again he paused. Then he looked up as if suddenly he had found his parents in a rifle sight. His voice was clear and certain. "I have to stay here, but I don't have to go to church."

Rob ran away from his parents' beliefs after one year at Central High School. Mentally, that is. Physically, he stayed at home through high school and a bit of college. But his heart was never really there after his freshman year.

"My parents talked about love, but they hated my new friends," Rob explains. "They would have family devotions and talk about how everyone was equal in God's sight, but my parents looked down on my friends who had little money. Bible discussions would focus on forgiveness, but every time I messed up, the punishment was tough, tough, tough. They were never wrong."

The sound of our kids' feet running away from our faith is deafening. But more than that, it's mind boggling!

The common fear of Christian parents

Some studies estimate that less than one-third of our students who are practicing Christians while they're in high school will still be practicing Christians when they graduate from college. We're losing about two-thirds of our kids after high school.

As Christian parents, this prospect scares us. Even a parent as godly as the apostle Paul seemed to have this fear. In 1 Thessalonians 3:5 Paul wrote these words to a group of people he considered his spiritual children: "When I could stand it no longer, I sent [Timothy] to find out about your faith. I was afraid that in some way the tempter might have tempted you and our efforts might have been useless."

Paul knew well how prone people are to drift away from the faith of their youth. In the last two letters he ever wrote Paul observed that people have a tendency to wander away from Christianity in a variety of ways.

He noticed that some leave *abruptly,* unexpectedly, as if victims of a terrible accident, as if they suddenly swerved off the road and smashed into a tree. It happened so fast that they didn't even have time to think about it.

Paul observed that other people leave in what seems a *single act of rebellion,* a decision to tear off the faith and throw it down. They're like Mark Twain's Tom Sawyer, who yanked off his shoes and threw them away as soon as his Aunt Polly wasn't looking.

Some of our teens act like they can't wait to tear off the faith they were made to wear as children.

Paul recognized that others experienced a *gradual process* of growing out of their faith. They got too big for the breeches that Christianity made them wear. They graduated or advanced out of the faith.

Our desperate plea

Paul's observations in 1 and 2 Timothy were written while he was in prison for his own commitment to Christ. He must have agonized in his cell as he received word of one fellow Christian after another dropping out of the faith (especially the ones whom he himself had led to Christ and spiritually parented). That made Paul wonder. Since people were so prone to wander away from the faith, how could he be sure that Christianity wouldn't die out after he did?

With this burning concern, Paul wrote to Timothy, his spiritual son, to show how their relationship was the prototype or blueprint for transmitting the Christian faith from one generation to the next.

Like Paul, we parents have a burning desire to see our love for God transmitted to our teenage children. However, in many homes, we aren't getting the message through.

Most of us blame ourselves when our teen starts to drift away from Christianity. Many times we're not doing anything wrong. Sometimes our kid is drifting because we're doing a lot of things right. But how can we know? How can we evaluate what we're doing and make the needed corrections unless we have a blueprint to follow?

Without a blueprint we have no place to turn when our teenager starts to drift. Note the words of one desperate father:

Dear Diary:

Today, I tried to spend some time with my teenage daughter. It was so hard just being with her . . . listening to her . . . watching how she handled herself. It made me ache inside.

When I was with her, I tried to tune into what she was feeling. I tried to share her very guarded space but, instead, found a glass wall. I could see her, but I wasn't allowed to get near her.

Nothing before has ever made me feel so sick. I guess that's the best word I can think of to describe how she made me feel. Just sick. I think it's a combination of different things—anger, shame, fear. All three hit my nervous system at once.

She wouldn't listen to anything I had to say. She was only interested in herself. It made me so angry.

I wanted to grab her and strangle her! I kept thinking: she knows better! What ever happened to the girl who once dedicated her life to tell the world about Christ?

It was easy, too, for me to feel angry at the youth workers from church who have worked with her. Why hadn't they reached out more to her?

Why hadn't I? Is her spiritual condition my fault? If so, I'm ashamed. What have I done to turn her off to Christ?

I'm told that everybody in the community is talking about her! When we go to church, I want to sneak in, sit in the back, then quietly sneak out.

What must other parents think as they hear the rumors about my daughter? They don't understand what it's like to have "evil" living in their own home. Just wait until it happens to them. They won't be so smug then!

My anger and shame is nothing compared to my fear, or should I say "terror"? I'm so afraid of the future. I'm afraid for my daughter. I'm scared to death she's going to hurt herself or others. Is she even a Christian? Would she go to hell if she died today? Sometimes I've thought and cried about this for hours.

I'm scared about my future too. What would life be like without my Christian daughter? No family times! No opportunity to be a grandparent. But, worst of all, I would have to live with myself—with this hole inside me, the sense of being a failure. It feels like I have lived my life for nothing!

Jesus said, "What profit is it if I gain the whole world but lose my soul?" I know I haven't lost my soul, but what profit would it be to gain the whole world but lose my daughter? My whole life would be purposeless if I leave behind a daughter who hates the God I love.

The question every teen must be allowed to ask

This father didn't know if his drifting daughter would ever come back. He experienced incredible agony as he watched her do what every teenager from a Christian home has to do—go back and reexamine the decisions she made to follow Christ when she was a child.

He felt helpless to control the outcome, and he really was. He couldn't control how his daughter was going to answer the question every Christian teen asks: "I know the kind of person my mom and dad want me to be, the kind of person that my church wants me to be. But what kind of person do I want to be?"

The healthier the home, the more openly kids can ask these questions. The less healthy the home, the more they have to keep secret their spiritual struggles. As they wrestle with these questions, our desperate plea to them should be the same as Paul's in his last letter to Timothy. "What you heard from me, keep as the pattern of sound teaching, with faith and love in Christ Jesus" (2 Timothy 1:13).

Paul's blueprint for life

In this one sentence, Paul used four different word pictures to communicate his deepest desire to Timothy, beginning with this phrase, *what you heard from me.*

Hearing

The Bible teaches that hearing is always the first stage in an individual's faith development. A life of faith begins with what kids "hear." That's why Paul pleads with Timothy to do something with what he heard from Paul.

The word Paul uses for *hear* signifies more than the hearing of sounds. It involves catching the meaning of a story, a song, or a play. Paul asked Timothy to remember the meaning he caught from watching Paul's life unfold.

The lives of all of us tell stories and communicate to others dozens of messages, intentionally and unintentionally. Our kids are bombarded with these conflicting messages every day. The ones they "hear" the most, and perhaps understand the most, are the verbal and nonverbal messages they get every day from us, their parents. Our teenagers are experts at "catching our drift" or hearing the hidden, unspoken meanings underneath our words.

Paul was well aware of what Timothy had "heard from him." However, we often are not aware of the messages we're sending our kids, especially messages about Christianity.

Keeping

Keep, the second word picture Paul uses here, means to grab on to or take hold. Paul used the same word twice in his first letter to Timothy. "Fight the good fight of the faith. *Take hold* of the eternal life to which you were called when you made your good confession. . . . Command those who are rich in this present world not to be arrogant or to put their hope in wealth . . . but to put their hope in God. . . . In this way . . . *take hold* of the life that is truly life" (1 Timothy 6:12, 17, 19, emphasis added).

When Paul urged Timothy to "take hold," he was using an active word. Taking hold is not just strolling over and casually picking up something. It's like a fish aggressively biting the bait and running with it.

A lot of us only nibble at Christianity like some fish nibble at a worm but never bite into it. Paul urged Timothy not to just nibble at Christianity. He sent the same kind of message we parents should be sending our teen: Remember all the messages you received from our lives. We want you to take hold of them now and run with them—like a fish would when it has finally decided it wants the bait.

The pattern of sound teaching

With this third word picture Paul tells Timothy not to treat these truths as casual information but rather as the only blueprint for life he could really trust. In essence, Paul was saying, "Son, you've been watching me live my life. I want you to take all that you've learned and heard from me and keep it as if it's the blueprint for life."

Our teen is desperately looking for something that will give him life. He's asking, "What do I have to do to make life work? What kind of person do I have to be to feel fully alive?" He's looking for a blueprint to show him where to find life.

Just like Paul, we need to live the kind of lives in front of our teen that say, "Don't grab onto any other blueprint than the one you've heard or learned from me. You really can trust the directions I've given you."

Most of us have had the experience of getting lost and having to ask strangers for directions. Sometimes these directions are reliable. Often they're not. However, the directions from a trusted friend are most reliable for reaching our destination.

Paul wanted Timothy to regard the "pattern of sound teaching" Paul had given him as a reliable blueprint from a trustworthy friend. "You take the blueprint I've given you and follow it as if your life depends on it because it really does! This is the only reliable blueprint for life."

With faith and love in Christ Jesus

Paul knew that only two things—faith and love—would motivate Timothy to keep following the blueprint he gave him. They're also the only two things that will motivate our teen to keep following the blueprint we give him.

All kids get a blueprint of some kind from their parents. As our teen tries to live by that blueprint, it seems to him, at times, that it's a blueprint that leads only to death.

"Dad, this is crazy. Nobody lives like this! Nobody does this stuff. Nobody handles problems like this. You're weird!"

In the face of these kinds of doubts, our pleas, pressure, or arguments will never be enough to motivate our kid to keep following the blueprint we give him.

Paul makes it clear that motivation is not a parent's responsibility. Our responsibility is, through our lives, to send our teen accurate messages about life and God. God's responsibility is to give our kid the faith and love that motivates him to "take hold" of the messages he hears from us.

What is a Christian parent's greatest task?

Our greatest task is to make sure our lives provide a reliable blueprint to the "life that is truly life."

Our task is not to make our teen listen

Often we parents mistakenly assume responsibility for things in our kid's life over which we have no control.

We often think, *If I could just get my teenager to listen to me. . . .* But we don't complete the sentence. What if we could get our kid to listen to us? Would that make him automatically obey us?

We must remember that listening is only the first step in our teen's spiritual development. Even if we could make him listen to us, that wouldn't change the kind of person he is on the inside.

When Paul wrote to Timothy, he assumed his protégé was listening to him all those years they traveled and worked together. Most of the time, it's safe to assume the same thing about our teen. He is often a better listener than we think. He not only hears our spoken messages, but our unspoken messages as well.

There's probably no information source that influences a kid more in his daily decisions than the messages he gets from his parents.

When we speak to our teenager, the first six words we say are the most important. He listens to those first six words and immediately judges what kind of message we're speaking. Is it a message he's already heard a thousand times? Is it relevant? Is it sincere? Is it worth "holding onto"?

Our teen studies us a whole lot more than we know. We're one of his favorite topics of thought and conversation—especially when life isn't going well for him.

Our responsibility is not to get our teen to listen to us. He probably already is listening. And even if he isn't, we really can't make him. Besides, when our messages aren't getting through, it's usually because something is wrong on the transmitting end, not the receiving end.

Our task is not to get our teen to take hold of something in life
Parents typically think, *I just wish I could get my kid to be committed to something. I wish I could get him excited about something, living for something.*

When we think this, we fail to recognize that a teenager is much like a drowning person. He will take hold of anything that looks like a life preserver. The problem is not that he refuses to take hold of anything, but that he has already taken hold of the wrong things.

Our teenager's generation is one of the most outspoken, articulate, obstinate, and opinionated generations of young people ever. They have taken hold of many things. They have stubborn convictions about where to find life. This is not an uncommitted generation. Today's kids know how to "keep" commitments. They know how to "take hold" of things with pit bull-like tenacity.

Paul's phrase "take hold" can also be translated "be addicted to." Our kid, in many ways, represents a generation of addicts—possibly more addicted to chemicals, material possessions, sensory experiences, and other people than any generation in history. This generation attaches itself to anything that promises life because it's a desperate and hungry generation. The problem with today's teens is not apathy. It's addiction! They have become addicted to things that really can't give them life at all.

Our task is not even to get our teen to take hold of Christianity
Many Christian parents assume that our greatest responsibility is to get our kid to take hold of Christianity, to get him to be a responsible, committed Christian. But what about the kid who has drifted away?

Usually, this kid has, at one time or another, openly taken hold of Christianity. He tried it but decided to give it up.

If we say our greatest responsibility is to get our teen to take hold of Christianity, what do we do when he gets disillusioned with that choice?

A teenager, by nature, is the purest kind of pragmatist. He is out to find something that works. A teen will usually give anything a try if someone tells him, "Hey, you ought to try this. It really makes me feel alive."

In most cases, a kid will even give Christianity a try—even take hold of it for a while if it does something for him. Getting a teenager to make a commitment to Christianity is not the hard part. The hard part is helping him find in Christianity something that will motivate him to give his life to it.

Our greatest task is to send our teen reliable, accurate messages about Christianity

Our responsibility as parents is not to get our kid to listen to us. It's not to get our kid to take hold of something. It's not even to get our kid to make a commitment to Christianity. Our responsibility is to send our kid, through our lives, a sound message about Christianity.

Imagine the cost of sending our teen an unsound, inaccurate message about Christianity. Our kid hears this message and believes it. So he tries it and finds out that it really isn't life. Now, what? We've left him disillusioned with what he mistakenly thinks is Christianity.

What are the chances we'll ever get him to try Christianity again? What are the chances he'll trust us again when we try to show him a different kind of Christianity?

So we need to look at what kind of information we're transmitting. More often than we know our teenager hears from us unintentional messages about Christianity that are not sound at all.

The message Steve heard

As a high school student, Steve was excited about Christianity. During his junior and senior years, he was one of the spiritual leaders in his youth group. He led prayer groups and Bible studies at school. He was the one who encouraged all the other Christian kids spiritually.

What a shock it was when, by his second year of college, Steve had completely left Christianity. At first, no one was sure what happened, but eventually the story came out.

Steve's dad was a pastor. Growing up, Steve watched his dad and decided Christianity was the best blueprint for success. That's why he put everything he had into Christianity when he was in high school.

He looked at his dad and saw the degrees on the wall, the people coming to him for counseling, a devoted group of people listening to him every Sunday. He saw his dad as one of the most successful people in the world. His dad said, "Son, this is the way to live. This is what life is all about."

Steve's dad thought he was teaching his son to live for Christ, but Steve was hearing his father say, "Live for success." Steve saw Christianity as a way to become successful and powerful.

That's how it worked for him for a while. Everything Steve did in high school turned to gold. A Christian in public high school, Steve was nevertheless successful and popular. But riding Christianity to success didn't work at college. He ran for freshman class president and lost. Then he began to have trouble with his grades. The more he failed, the harder he prayed. When God didn't help him get better grades, he grew increasingly disillusioned.

Why isn't Christianity working for me anymore? he wondered. He prayed more and increased his church involvement, but more disappointments followed. None of the girls he was interested in were interested in him. And some of the guys in his dorm were now starting to give him a hard time about being a Christian. He felt more isolated and depressed.

At that point Steve concluded that Christianity wasn't a reliable blueprint to popularity and success. He felt deceived by his parents and other Christians. He decided to follow some other blueprints—the types of blueprints that seemed to be helping the other kids at the university.

As Steve grew up, no one knew about the erroneous message he was hearing. He came to view Christianity as the blueprint for something it wasn't, because he heard his father and others at church saying, "Be a Christian and you'll be successful just like us."

Steve is typical. Often, an adolescent chooses the "Christian road" thinking it's the road to success, power, or popularity—something Christianity is not! Then, after traveling on that road for a few years and finding it doesn't get him there, the teen becomes disillusioned and changes routes. When we try to call him back, all our kid hears is an invitation to return to the same dead-end road that took him away from what he really wanted.

A different message for Rachel

As a high school student, Rachel was very involved in the church youth group. Within months after high school graduation, she gave up her faith. Why?

Rachel grew up in a single-parent home, and her mom seemed like a devout Christian woman; she never missed a Sunday at church. However, Rachel's mom didn't realize the message Rachel was hearing as she grew up.

All through high school, Rachel had watched her mother struggle with low self esteem and chronic depression despite her active involvement in Christian activities. Listening carefully, Rachel was hearing a message that her mother didn't even know she was sending: "Christianity alone is not enough. If you don't have a man, life isn't complete."

As a teenager, Rachel discovered that Christianity was no help in getting high school boys interested in her. In many settings, her Christian standards made it harder to get a boyfriend. When she went to college, she finally shed Christianity because it seemed to be holding her back. She vowed never to live the unhappy life her mother modeled for her. As soon as she discarded her Christian standards, guys began to show her more attention, which reinforced her decision.

Rachel walked away from Christianity because she concluded from watching her mother that Christianity was not the blueprint for real life. Finding a man was.

Our teen isn't hearing what we think he's hearing

Like Steve and Rachel, our teen will pick up messages from us and other Christians that were never actually spoken.

A teen often leaves Christianity because he becomes disillusioned listening to other Christians' distorted, inaccurate messages about Christianity—a Christianity that isn't true Christianity at all.

The incredible listening ability of our teen

An adolescent has listening skills a child doesn't have: both the skills to tune things out and the skills to pick things up.

Tuning out the insincere

A teen can pick up an insincere message within six words and tune it out in a snap. He takes what we say and measures it against what he sees us doing. If we're not consistent, he concludes we're not sincere.

When a teenager has no opportunity to observe his Sunday school teacher outside of class, he automatically assumes that what his teacher says is insincere. Since most adults he encounters are insincere, he's reluctant to give the benefit of the doubt to an adult he doesn't know. This might seem prejudicial, but experience has taught him to be skeptical of adults.

So, any of us who want to be effective with our teen must let him see us in informal settings. That's why we as parents often have the best opportunity of any Christian to send messages to our kid that he'll listen to. We have more contact in informal settings with our teenager than any other adult.

The youth pastor's conflicting message

During a devotional time with the high school group one Sunday night, a youth pastor taught a lesson designed to encourage teens to commit themselves to loving other people.

He hammered at this theme for over an hour and even suggested the group be called Agape (a Greek word for love).

After the meeting, everyone drove through the rain to McDonald's. On the way, as the youth pastor's car passed a man changing a flat tire, one of his passengers said, "We ought to stop and help him."

"We don't have time now," the youth pastor responded. "We have to meet the others." Nothing else was said, and they drove on.

Several weeks went by, and the youth pastor started wondering why his message about love didn't seem to be getting through to the kids. They weren't reaching out to their friends, taking interest in missions opportunities, or signing up for a new course on "people helping" offered at the church. The youth pastor approached one of his key kids and asked him what the problem was.

"Well, we figure you didn't really mean all that stuff about love since you wouldn't even stop and help that guy with the flat tire."

The kids decided that if their youth pastor's life didn't match his spoken message, everything else he said was insincere. They tuned it all out. Each of our kids has an incredible ability to detect and tune out insincere messages.

Tuning out angry messages

As soon as someone (especially an adult) starts to get angry with a teen, the kid turns his hearing aid down. He believes that any directions we give him when we're angry aren't accurate, helpful, or reliable. So, why take them seriously? Angry messages, he's discovered, aren't blueprints to life at all. They're usually blueprints to death.

Tuning out the extraneous

A teen is also good at tuning out messages that aren't relevant. A potential drowning victim pays attention only to messages that tell him how to keep his head above the water, like, "Hey, there's a rope behind you. Grab it."

Too often our teen perceives us as standing on shore, scolding him for being in a drowning situation. It's like we're yelling, "What in the world did you do to get yourself in this situation, anyway? Apparently, you were breaking some rule. I think it's important, before we pull you out, to talk about how we can keep this from happening again."

Our kid feels like he's drowning! He's gasping for air! Naturally, he's going to tune out extraneous messages.

While our kid is skilled at tuning certain messages out, he is equally skilled at picking up certain kinds of messages.

Tuning in the unspoken

Remember the unspoken message of Rachel's mom: "Since my life and worth as a woman depends on a relationship with a man and I don't have one, I'll settle for what little consolation being a Christian will give me."

How different that message was from the spoken message she was giving Rachel. However, our unspoken messages usually have far more influence on our teenager than our spoken messages do.

Picking up the unintended

The youth group watched their leader ignore a person in need (fixing a flat tire in the rain). Although he didn't realize it, through this action he was saying, "It's more important to build our youth group than to love people. It's more important to keep your parents from getting angry with me for getting you home late than it is to love people." That wasn't the message he intended to communicate. But that's what they heard.

What teens hear the best

The messages our kid hears the best are passionate ones. Our teenager studies us to see which events, people, or things make us look and act most alive—the ones that fill us with passion.

From this, he concludes where we're finding our source of life. It doesn't matter so much what we tell him. What matters is where and how he sees us come alive with passion. Then he says, "I've been wondering all these years where Dad finds life. So that's it!"

Our teen looks for the passion in our lives

Passion gets our kid's attention. Just before Paul was executed, he described his passion to Timothy, his son in the faith. "I am already being poured out like a drink offering, and the time has come for my departure. I have fought the good fight. I have finished the race. I have kept the faith" (2 Timothy 4:6–7).

Just like Paul, we as parents pour our lives into whatever we believe will give us life. That's why our kid studies us— not so much for the words we speak but for the passion we display. He listens to our voice inflections, our tone, our nonverbal communication, to see when we become most animated. This is how he measures our passion.

What message do you suppose our teen hears when the most passion he sees in us is when we bring home a new car? He says, "I've never seen Dad giggle like a little boy before, but when he got that car and drove it in the driveway, he became alive. And man, you ought to see how he pours his heart into keeping that car spotless! A lot of things may not get done on the weekends, but Dad's car always gets waxed. Once, when his new car got scratched, he got so angry! I never saw him get more angry about anything else in the world than he did about his car."

Does this dad have any idea what message he's giving his son? The son's not hearing what the father thinks he's hearing. The son hears, "Just get to a point in life where you can own a car like this—a car that can make people's heads turn—and that's where you'll find life."

What message do you think our kid gets when the only time Mom gets passionate—her voice goes up and she gets really excited—is when she hears news about someone that she can pass on to others. Unfortunately, it's usually negative news about people she doesn't like. The teen thinks: *Gossip is Mom's source of life, the purpose that makes her life worth living.*

The fact that she goes to church every Sunday and occasionally reads her Bible will say very little to him compared to the volumes her passion teaches. Passion speaks more loudly than anything else to a kid.

At some time or another every teenager tries out for himself whatever his mom or dad show the most passion about. If it doesn't really lead to life, he casts it away like a pair of shoes that don't fit. Then he starts looking to other people outside his home to point him to a truer source of life. He may never again trust his parents to be a reliable guide when it comes to the vital stuff.

Two questions for reflective parents

It's essential for us as Christian parents to honestly reflect on what our kid might be hearing from us. Honest reflection begins by asking ourselves two key questions.

Question #1: *How can I know what kind of messages my teen is hearing from me?*

After asking himself this question Dan decided to ask his daughter what she thought was the most important lesson he wanted her to learn about life.

She replied, "Work hard, do your best and don't lie."

His daughter's answer perplexed him. *I wonder why my children apparently do not see the pursuit of love as the cen-*

tral purpose of life, he thought. *Perhaps love is so rare, even in good homes, that other lessons about life are preeminent in the classroom of family living.* *

By simply asking, Dan discovered that his daughter was not hearing what he thought he was conveying. Maybe that's a good place for all of us to start. Maybe we could even borrow Dan's question to his daughter: "What do you think is the most important lesson I want you to learn about life?"

So, one way to discover what our kid is hearing from us is to simply ask him. If he answers us honestly, it will be our best clue to what messages our lives are sending him.

What if we asked a question similar to Dan's and our teen replied that he thought being a Christian meant "just being a nice person"? What if this had gone undetected? Our teen would have carried into adult life the belief that "Life depends on being a really nice person. That's where life is found." Then what would our teen be forced to conclude about Christianity before he even got out of his twenties? A simple question like this can detect problems and give us the opportunity to correct a destructive impression we may have given our kid about Christianity. Asking direct questions, though, is not the only way we can find out what our teen hears us saying.

A second way to discover what our kid is hearing from us is to listen closely to what he's saying. Proverbs says, "A fool's mouth is his undoing, his lips are a snare to his soul" (18:7).

All we have to do is listen to a teenager talk long enough, and he'll tell us where he's trying to find life. Often it won't be in his relationship with Christ.

The most important thing to listen for is passion. Just as our teen studies us for passion, we should study him for passion. When do we hear the most passion in his voice?

---

*Dan B. Allender, *The Courageous Practice of Life's Ultimate Influence* (Colorado Springs: NavPress, 1993), 35–36.

One teen may display the most passion when she gets new clothes. What does that say about what she thinks is the source of life? Another teen might come alive (really alive!) whenever his girlfriend calls.

Isn't that typical of a teenager? Sure. But even more, it's typical of immaturity. The question is, Is he learning this immature view—that life is in new clothes or in girlfriends— by watching us? As reflective parents, we have to ask ourselves that question. Is he learning to be passionate about the wrong things by watching us?

A third way to discover what our kid is hearing from us is to observe him. What does he pursue that we pursue? What passions of ours does he share? A passion for sports? Nice things? Education? Fun? This is one of the best indicators we have of the kind of gospel he's hearing from us.

How can we know what our teen is really hearing from us? Ask him. Listen to him. Observe him with an open mind. The answer will often prompt a second question.

Question #2: *What do we do when our kid is getting messages from us that we don't want him to get?*

When we discover that our kid is "hearing us wrong," we naturally want to take quick action. Sometimes the actions we take, however, are destructive.

Destructive responses

Sometimes we **criticize** our kid for not hearing what we want him to hear. Consider this conversation:

"That's not what I taught you about life!"

"But you said . . ."

"No, I didn't mean that!"

"But Dad, you get upset about that stuff all the time."

"I never get upset!"

If our kid is hearing messages we don't want him to hear from our lives, we can't change his mind by criticizing him and saying he is really the problem.

Sometimes, we just **turn up the volume** on our spoken message when we're around our teen. If the message we want him to get isn't getting through, we shout it louder. We forget that the louder we speak, the angrier we sound. This makes it even more likely that our teen will tune us out.

Other times we try to improve our messages by **improving our spiritual performance around our kid.** If our kid is hearing us say that life depends on making our house into a shrine because he sees us pouring more energy into shrubs, lawns, and interior decorating than we do anything else, then it's easy to decide to spend less time on the house and more time in Bible studies.

Before we jump to this conclusion, though, consider what new message this will send. Our teen might hear us saying, "Life depends upon our being real busy—at church instead of at home." Is this message any better?

The Pharisees followed the spiritual performance blueprint. How did they do? Christ condemned them for it. We must not think we can change our message to our kid by just improving our spiritual performance.

Creative Responses

If we want to avoid actions that are destructive, what can we do when we find out our kid is getting messages we don't want him to get?

Look at ourselves.

The only way to begin making fundamental changes in the messages our lives send to our teen is to ask ourselves some hard questions: "Where do we go to find life? What things are we the most passionate about?"

When we ask ourselves these questions, we discover things that trouble us. Maybe we're too seldom passionate about what we thought was most important to us. Maybe our kid sees us more passionate about making money or being important or even playing sports than we are about our relationship with Christ.

Ask others.

We shouldn't rely only on our own answers to these questions either. How will our closest friends answer if we ask them where they see the most passion in our lives?

Turn to God.

Once we become aware of misplaced passion and misleading messages in our lives, there is nothing we can do to change them on our own. Our only hope for change is to ask God to do something with our hearts that we cannot do for ourselves—to create in us the kind of heart that only seeks life in Him—to give us a heart that sings as the psalmist's did when he wrote, "As the deer pants for streams of water, so my soul pants for you, O God" (Psalm 42:1).

Our teen's reaction

Be prepared. This kind of change in us will stir up questions and confusion in our kid. People questioned the psalmist when they saw his passion for God. "Why are you so passionate about God?" they asked. "Where is the evidence that he's worth that much trouble?"

In the same way our kid will start to question us. The new message he hears will greatly puzzle him. That's good. Our kid ought to be puzzled when he begins to see his parents' passion shift. He doesn't see that kind of change in people very often.

Eventually his confusion will turn to curiosity. At that point, he might even be interested in trying for himself this new source of life he sees in us. Remember, however, the messages our hearts send out to our kid can't possibly be changed until our hearts are changed. And that's a work God does only when He's invited.

Paul's passions sent a strong message to Timothy. "You . . . know all about my teaching, my way of life, my purpose, faith, patience, love, endurance, persecutions, [and] sufferings" (2 Timothy 3:10).

It's as if Paul were saying, "All I can ask, son, as I'm on my deathbed, is that you pour your passion and your energies into the same thing I poured mine into, trusting me that this is the life that is truly life."

To be in a position to call our teen to this kind of life, we must ask God to give us hearts like Paul's. The quality of our hearts determine the quality of our message.

Two

Why Our Teen's Faith Doesn't Last

Samantha's mother stood up and announced that she was ready to talk about her daughter's death. The twenty-five friends and family who had come to her house were ready for some answers.

They, along with hundreds of others, had sat through funeral services at the church and cemetery. Both services had been frustrating because Christian burials are usually triumphant. But Samantha's had been exactly the opposite. Everyone who had known Samantha was shaken, confused, and completely stunned.

Those who had witnessed Samantha and her boyfriend signing a public pledge to say no to premarital sex wondered why her last night on earth had included a very public orgy-like display of promiscuous behavior.

Others who had assisted her in community antidrinking activities couldn't reconcile the fact that she had twice the legal limit of alcohol in her bloodstream that fatal night.

Even more confused were those friends who had heard her antidrug speeches: "God wants us to keep our bodies pure and clean." Yet she had been using a deadly combination of three heavy drugs in toxic doses when she died.

Then the final kicker. Apparently, this behavior was not a first. One of her "friends" who survived said, "We've been on this ride since July."

With these inconsistencies in mind, a small group gathered at Samantha's usually fun-filled family room to ask why.

Samantha's mother struggled to explain. "All her life Samantha stood for something. But her life ended with her going against everything she ever stood for."

"Why did she walk away from her beliefs?" a heartbroken adult asked. "Why did she reject her Christianity?"

Samantha's mother had no answer, but she tried. "Maybe it was this summer. She spent almost the entire three months with our friends at the shore. When she got home for her senior year, she seemed so different. It was as if she drifted out to sea, drifted so far away that she couldn't find her way back."

Why are we so prone to drift away from Christianity—especially when we're young?

Five kinds of drifters

In his letters to Timothy, Paul warned about five different groups of drifters. On the surface these groups looked similar. Each had left their outward identification with Christ, but they did it for different reasons.

During adolescence, many high school and college students drift, too, for many reasons. Each of the groups Paul observed centuries ago can still be found among our young people today. This is why parents must pay close attention to the instructions Paul gave Timothy about drifters.

Deserters

Paul described the first and largest group of drifters as deserters. Deserters leave their outward identification with Christ and his church in pursuit of a more comfortable existence than what Christianity offers. They are looking for something more physically and emotionally satisfying.

In 1 Timothy 5:5 Paul says that lonely people are the most susceptible to deserting. He used widows as an example. "The widow who is really in need and left all alone puts her hope in God and continues night and day to pray and to ask God for help. But the widow who lives for pleasure is dead even while she lives."

These are the same two options our teenage sons and daughters today have for coping with loneliness: pursue God or pursue pleasure.

Live for pleasure and be dead even while they live, is a phrase that characterizes too many teenagers today. Even some who are involved in Christian activities make this choice.

To put their hope in an invisible God and find strength and comfort from Him to endure isolation, loneliness, and despair requires a personal faith most teenagers haven't had time to develop yet.

That's why so many opt for deserting Christianity and living for pleasure. Instead of finding relief, however, they find only a kind of "walking deadness." Paul explained more about deserters in verses 11 and 12. He says, "When their sensual desires overcome their dedication to Christ, they want to marry. Thus they bring judgment on themselves, because they have broken their first pledge."

When a teen deserts Christianity, it's because her sensual desires have overcome her dedication to Christ. This doesn't necessarily mean that she doesn't believe in Christ anymore, only that she believes more in something else. She believes that her life can be better fulfilled through the pursuit of pleasure than through the pursuit of Christ. Since it's impossible to pursue both at the same time, she abandons her pursuit of Christ.

Many times, when kids first encounter Christianity, they get the impression that Christ promises them a comfortable existence if they follow Him. Many churches deliberately communicate this to teenagers.

Bridget deals with loneliness—and deserts

Bridget was a high school student whose dad had left many years before. Her mom worked so many hours that Bridget was home alone most of the time.

One weekend, as she was walking by a church near her home, she saw a group of high schoolers in the parking lot playing crazy games. She wandered over, and the kids quickly invited her to join them. That day, she found a warmth and acceptance she had never experienced before. Over the next several months, the church became her family. Eventually, she dedicated her life to Christ and joined the church. All through high school, Bridget was one of the most faithful and dedicated members of the church's youth group.

As these kids reached college age, all developed steady dating relationships—all except Bridget. Being almost a hundred pounds overweight severely limited her dating potential. Bridget's feelings of rejection and loneliness grew, especially around the other kids at church. Going to church no longer relieved her loneliness. It added to it.

About this time, a non-Christian man at the college she attended started dating Bridget. She found herself deeply involved in a relationship which required her to make a choice about her Christianity. As a devout Muslim, this man pressured her to abandon her faith. "I really want to marry you but I can't if you are a practicing Christian," he told her.

In the end, Bridget married this man. She left her outward identification with Christ and His people in search of something she hadn't found in Christianity—male companionship and potential for the family she always wanted. Motivated by a core commitment that superseded all others, Bridget became a deserter.

Paul identified the core commitment of a deserter. He told Timothy, "Do your best to come to me quickly, for Demas, *because he loved this world,* has deserted me" (2 Timothy 4:9–10, emphasis added).

The highest commitment of deserters is to find, from the world instead of Christ, what they think they need for life. That's why they love the world more than Christ. Although for a while deserters may find what they want around Christianity, sooner or later, they always find the world's offers more appealing. When the sacrifices Christianity requires become too great, they trade their allegiance to Christ for allegiance to another cause or person that promises greater satisfaction.

Disputers

While deserters drift away from Christianity because they're looking for something more physically or emotionally satisfying, disputers drift in search of something more intellectually satisfying. Disputers leave their outward identification with Christ and His body of believers in pursuit of a way of life that makes more sense to them, that offers a way out of the confusion they feel.

As kids move into adolescence and begin to acquire adult thinking capacities, they begin to see huge inconsistencies between what Christians preach and what they practice.

They also notice seeming contradictions in Bible doctrines. How can a God of love control everything yet allow war, poverty, and child abuse?

When reality seems to contradict the teachings of Christianity, a disputer wants to replace Christianity with a new brand of truth.

World-traveler Tom

Tom grew up as a pastor's son. He had opportunities to observe Christianity inside and out. He was around it his whole life. He had traveled with his father all over the world and seen Christianity at work in Africa, Europe, and South America. As Tom moved into his college years, many things troubled him. He couldn't reconcile the fact that so many people who said they were Christians conducted their relationships with such disregard.

Tom had seen many people in churches hurt each other and mistreat his own father and mother. It made him want to dispute Christianity, dismiss it as a hoax.

"People who only pretend to love, serve nothing more than a pretend God," he often said.

On Tom's travels around the world, he'd seen so much poverty and hunger—children starving to death—that he could not reconcile this with a God of love.

By his second year of college, Tom decided to leave Christianity in pursuit of some kind of system or philosophy that would better explain what he saw as reality. He wanted to find anything he could to dispute Christianity.

Whenever kids start to intellectually drift, as Tom did, sooner or later they end up morally drifting too. Tom's search for new truth led him deeper into despair. In the end, Tom's only relief from confusion was to stay as high as he could on drugs.

Paul described the disputer in 2 Timothy 4:3–4: "For the time will come when men will not put up with sound doctrine. Instead, to suit their own desires, they will gather around them a great number of teachers to say what their itching ears want to hear. They will turn their ears away from the truth and turn aside to myths."

Why do disputers drift? To soothe their desires, to scratch their itching ears, to get away from the claims of Christianity and the tensions those claims cause. Disputers challenge God's truth and invent their own, thinking they can create a more just and reasonable universe for themselves. In the end, however, they only create more chaos.

Deceivers

These individuals come into churches or youth groups disguised as sincere Christians in order to take advantage of unsuspecting or weak Christians. Here is how Paul described deceivers:

> They are the kind who worm their way into homes [and churches] to gain control over weak-willed women [or men or teenagers], who are loaded down with sins and swayed by all kinds of evil desires. . . . They will not get very far because, as in the case of those men, their folly will be clear to everyone. . . . [These] evil men and impostors will go from bad to worse, deceiving and being deceived (2 Timothy 3:6, 9, 13).

Deceivers, according to Paul, are people who temporarily seek outward identification with Christ and His body in pursuit of partners in pleasure. They seek to pull the weaker members of our churches and youth groups into exploitative relationships. While deserters go outside the church to find sensual fulfillment, deceivers work inside it.

Jerry's agenda

Jerry, a high school junior, started attending church because somebody from school invited him. The church had a small youth group of about twenty junior high and high school students, mostly girls. Naturally, the girls were very happy to see another guy join the group.

After only a few weeks, Jerry made a profession of faith in Christ. He started to get very involved and attended every meeting.

In a few more weeks, though, Jerry's real reason for joining the group became apparent. Before long, he was pursuing every girl that he could get near. There were rumors he was even pressuring girls to have sex with him.

When some of the youth group leaders questioned Jerry about the rumors, he admitted that the only reason he came to church was because he liked the girls. "This church has a reputation for having the best girls in town."

Later, the leaders found out that this was the third or fourth youth group Jerry had exploited. He would leave each group only after his real agenda was exposed.

Jerry was the kind of deceiver Paul warned Timothy about. He had sought identification with Christ and His people only to use them to get what he wanted.

Deceivers can be individuals who grow up in the church and keep hanging around because that's where they'll find the best company for doing evil. When they are finally exposed and leave, it appears that they've drifted away from the faith. According to Paul, however, all along they were "missing true faith." They were merely pretending.

Dominators

Dominators are people who temporarily seek outward identification with Christ and His body in the pursuit of power or influence. They strive to be spiritual leaders in the church or youth group because, more than anything else, they want to be in a position of power over others. Look at what Paul says about this group: "Some have wandered away from [God's work] and turned to meaningless talk. They want to be teachers of the law, but they do not know what they are talking about or what they so confidently affirm" (1 Timothy 1:6–7).

Dominators identify with Christ and His people for what they can personally gain from being part of the Christian community. Even adolescents can be dominators. They publicly identify with Christ and His body because they're looking for control, power, or influence.

Jo-Lynn joins the group

The kids were excited when one of the most popular girls at high school began to attend their youth group. Her name was Jo-Lynn. She was part of the "in group" at school.

Immediately she rose to the top and was made one of the youth group officers. The adult leaders loved her because she really knew how to make things happen. She could charm anybody into doing anything for her.

It was a shock when, after just four or five months, Jo-Lynn dropped out of the youth group, coincidentally after she was elected homecoming queen.

Nobody could understand what was wrong. Had someone hurt her feelings? Finally, when a couple of the kids cornered her at school, Jo-Lynn admitted she wasn't interested in being a part of the youth group anymore. She told them she only got involved in the group to get votes for homecoming queen. Since theirs was the biggest youth group in town, she decided to use it as a place to pick up more votes.

Jo-Lynn identified with the group just to get a little bit of power and influence.

Matt, the super-Christian

Matt was also a dominator. All through high school, he was the one who led the Bible studies at school and youth group.

Matt was made superintendent over the entire Sunday school when he was a senior in high school. Sometimes, on Sundays when the pastor was away, church officials would even ask him to fill the pulpit! Everybody thought Matt was destined to be a preacher.

When he graduated from high school, Matt went to a university and immediately got involved in a campus ministry.

However, he quickly lost interest when he found out that the director would not allow him to be a Bible study leader for at least two semesters. The ministry's policy required everyone to go through some steps of discipleship and training before serving in a leadership capacity.

Angry that he could not be a leader, Matt dropped out, not only out of that ministry but out of Christian activities altogether.

Those who knew Matt in high school sought him out when they heard what had happened. But Matt had already replaced his church involvement with fraternity activities. In the fraternity, Matt didn't have to wait to get into a position of leadership.

"I don't need Christianity anymore," said Matt. "I've got my fraternity." He then explained that his fraternity, the most prestigious and influential on campus, planned to back his campaign for a student government office.

Like Matt, dominators identify with Christ and His people only as long as it provides the authority and power they're pursuing. This is why it is dangerous to make our kid a "spiritual celebrity." It becomes easy for teens to conclude that the purpose of Christianity is self-aggrandizement. They may think, "Hey, this spiritual stuff is OK. It really gets people to look up to me."

Later, they discover that's not what Christianity is all about, and they feel deceived or cheated. Just as Matt did, they start to move angrily away from Christianity in search of greener pastures.

The Defeated

In the wake of some kind of moral failure, defeated individuals leave Christianity because they feel ashamed. They usually try to leave before anybody finds out and has a chance to expose them. This is the kid who says, "I tried being a Christian but I just can't live up to it."

Dave and John—friends but not forever

Dave and John were two high school friends—a little like the Biblical friends, David and Jonathan. In high school they accepted Christ at the same time. For about two months, Dave and John pioneered the Christian life together. They prayed about everything, studied the Bible, and talked about it constantly.

Dave was very concerned about two or three areas of his life that he was constantly asking John to pray about. Dave had been going with a girl named Dara for about two years before he had accepted Christ, and they had become sexually active. He felt that since he now was a Christian, they shouldn't have any kind of physical relationship. It was a major struggle whenever he and Dara were together.

Dave was also concerned about his habits of cigarette smoking and masturbating. He thought that if he was any kind of Christian at all, he ought to be able to break these habits.

After trying for about two months to get control of these three areas of his life, he went to John one day and said, "John, it's just too hard! I can't do it. I can't keep trying to live like a Christian. I'm quitting. I can't live with all the guilt and shame. I can't stand it."

John did his best to talk Dave out of it, to show him that God would help him with these things and that they were something Dave didn't need to run away from.

But Dave couldn't stand failure. He had always been successful at anything he attempted. Christianity was the first area in which he couldn't succeed. It drove him crazy.

He was the quarterback on the high school team—the best football player in the county—he had the prettiest girl in school, he had close to a 4.0 grade point average, and had been accepted to one of the Ivy League schools.

Everything Dave touched turned to gold. Everything but Christianity, that is. He felt disgraced. Not wanting to live with that kind of shame anymore, he decided to bail out.

Paul alerted Timothy about this pattern repeating itself, especially in new Christians. That's why he counseled Timothy to be careful whom he appointed as leaders in the church. "He must not be a recent convert, or he may become conceited and fall under the same judgment as the devil. He must also have a good reputation with outsiders, so that he will not fall into disgrace and into the devil's trap" (1 Timothy 3:6–7).

Often, new Christians become overconfident about all the new changes in their lives and begin to take credit for these changes. In their pride, they drift away from Christ and eventually fall back into sinful practices. When this happens, they feel so defeated and embarrassed—just as Dave did— that they walk away from Christianity.

What every parent should know about drifters

Drifters, on the surface, often look alike. They stop coming around the church. They get involved in practices and pursuits that are not associated with Christianity. However, beneath the surface, drifters can differ greatly in why they wander away.

A deserter drifts away for a different reason than a disputer, deceiver, dominator, or defeated kid.

That's why we have to be careful before we jump to conclusions about teens who start to leave Christianity. We must look into what actually led them away from their outward identification with Christ.

Parents often wonder, *If my teen drifts, does it mean she never was a Christian at all? Or is she a prodigal Christian, destined to return someday? How does drifting affect her eternal salvation?*

Paul doesn't answer these questions in so many words. He seems to imply that deceivers and dominators never had faith to begin with. But the conclusion is not clear for deserters, disputers, and the defeated.

However, it is clear that we parents must recognize when our kid starts to drift and respond in a way that encourages her to return. This requires a working knowledge of six truths that characterize all drifters.

Characteristic #1: *Drifters are rebels.* Underlying the actions of every drifter is a heart in rebellion against God. Drifters believe that they can satisfy their basic needs on their own rather than by trusting Christ.

Every human being has been created by God to experience three things: warmth (love), height (recognition or importance) and weight (power or control).

Deserters and **deceivers** are looking for warmth—people to love and care about them. Deserters go outside the church to find this, yet deceivers sneak inside the church.

Disputers are looking for weight—a religion or philosophy that provides them a greater sense of control and predictability over their world.

Dominators are looking for height and weight—situations in which they can stand above others and tell them what to do.

Defeated drifters run because they fear losing height and warmth when their failures become known in the church.

All drifters are guilty of putting their own interests before Christ's. When confronted with the choice to serve Christ or serve themselves, they'll always choose to serve themselves.

Characteristic #2: *Drifters are susceptible to being "pushed" or "pulled" away from Christianity when the right event comes along.* "Push" events turn a person off to Christ or to the church. "Pull" events turn a person on to the world—

making the world irresistibly attractive. These two types of events trigger drifting in teenagers.

Sarah's going to shine this year!

Sarah was in her senior year at a Christian high school. Although there were only seventy-nine in her class, she had never been part of the "in crowd." For three years, she had been limited socially, mostly by her own cautious personality. Sarah resolved that her senior year would be different.

It's my turn to bloom, she thought. *I'm a senior this year. I'm going to parties. I'm going to get a part in the school play. I'm going to have a steady boyfriend. Look out, here I come!*

Sarah's parents went along. They helped her buy her own car. They changed her curfew to 1:00 A.M. They began to host parties for Sarah's friends after the football games.

It was like a dream come true for Sarah. She was starting to be accepted by the most popular group in the school. She was welcomed with open arms into every extracurricular activity she pursued. Her grades remained high with little or no effort. And she was dating one of the most popular football players in school.

Everyone seemed to be cooperating with her plan— even God. Since Sarah had been a good kid her whole life, she figured that this was God's way of rewarding her.

Sarah's parents were delighted with all these new developments in their daughter's life. Having worried about "the shell" she'd been living in, they were excited to watch her blossoming during her senior year.

Sarah's (and her parents') dream, however, soon vaporized. At a party following the last football game of the season, several of the seniors, including Sarah, got drunk. When parents and school officials found out, they were outraged.

The following week, the school administration expelled three seniors and suspended nine.

Despite her remorse and her parents' appeals, Sarah was one of the students expelled. The football players who brought the beer to the party were suspended for only a few weeks. One of them was her boyfriend.

Sarah knew the boys received only suspensions because they were expected to be the stars on the basketball team that year, the very year the school had its best chance in a decade to win the conference championship.

The basketball team did go on to become conference champs. Sarah, who had to finish the last half of her senior year in another school, never attended a game.

The boy she had been dating returned from his suspension in time to break both the school and conference scoring records. He never called Sarah again. She heard that he started dating one of the cheerleaders. He was even awarded a scholarship to a Christian college famous as a basketball powerhouse.

This incident became a *push* event for Sarah. Embittered by it, she spent the rest of her senior year just going through the motions—being a good girl again on the outside while on the inside her heart hardened against God and His people.

After graduation, Sarah attended a state university and quickly severed all ties with her Christian friends and church family. Despite pleas from her parents, Sarah looked to a New Age movement on campus for the warmth and height she felt God and Christians had denied her.

While the event that triggered Sarah's desertion from Christianity was a "push" event, for other kids the triggering event is often a "pull" event. This happens when the world makes teens an offer that seems too attractive to refuse. The world's offers appear much more satisfying than those of the church or God.

The pull away from Christianity seems almost irresistible. Remember the pull Bridget felt when a non-Christian man offered her the male companionship she couldn't find in the church?

We must prepare our teen to withstand push and pull events. The key to discouraging drifting in our teenager is not to try to insulate her from experiencing push or pull events.

We couldn't do it even if we tried. We can never find a church or group of Christians that could keep from disappointing or disillusioning our teen. We can't prevent cancer, accidents, or man-made disasters from invading her world from time to time. Any of these can push our kid to leave Christianity.

We can't insulate our kid from attractive offers from the world, either—promises to deliver everything she's always wanted. Quarantining our kid from all the deceptive and seductive influences in this world is impossible. We have to find a better strategy.

The key to discouraging drifting in our teen is to assail whatever it is in her heart that predisposes her to drift when the right push or pull event comes along. What makes teens susceptible to drifting is the whole direction of their lives.

Characteristic #3: *The direction of drifters' lives takes them on a path through Christianity rather than into it.*

Drifters view Christianity as a stepping stone to something else instead of a destination. They use the Christian faith to get something they want.

Christianity is used to accomplish or attain things that have nothing to do with the real work or life of Christ. There's probably nothing more misused or exploited in this world.

Those who use Christianity to achieve their own agendas will always be predisposed to drifting when a better offer comes along. A kid may use Christianity to find success, to get the family she never had, or to become popular.

Such goals set kids up to drift away from Christianity as soon as the conditions are right because their goal permits them to stay committed to Christianity only as long as it gives them what they want most.

Characteristic #4: *Drifters have a surface commitment to give Christianity a chance.*

We read in 1 Timothy 1:7 that certain people were using Christianity because they wanted to be teachers of the law. They wanted to be somebody important. Many times teens give Christianity a chance, too, just to see if it will make them into the kind of person they want to be instead of who God wants them to be.

Remember John's friend, Dave? He was committed to being competent in everything. He thought that Christianity would just be one more thing that would make him a cut above other people. When he tried Christianity, he found out that it exposed his real incompetencies—his moral failures.

He couldn't master Christianity like he could master football and everything else, so he gave it up. He made a surface commitment to Christianity for two months to try it out, to see if it gave him what he wanted, to find out if it made him who he wanted to be.

All teenagers, like Dave, have in mind a picture of who they want to be, the person they think they have to be to get what they want out of life.

Sometimes a kid approaches Christianity thinking it will help her close the gap between the person she is now and the person she wants to be. We might call it the gap between her real self and her ideal self.

In order to close the gap, she may start going to church, reading the Bible, and doing everything that Christianity asks her to do. Soon she finds out that, instead of the gap closing, the gap only widens. The ugly, sinful parts of her soul are exposed by Christ's teachings. She discovers how hard it is to live the way God wants her to.

The more a kid reads the Bible, the more her eyes are opened to how far she is from the person God wants her to be. She starts to think, *I'm not into anything that makes me feel bad about myself. I'm only into things that make me feel better about myself, things like weight-loss diets or good friends or more education or whatever it is. If it makes me feel better about myself, I'm into it. But this Christianity stuff—the longer I'm into it the more I dislike myself.*

This is often why teens wander away from the faith. Their surface commitment to Christianity is dwarfed by a much larger commitment to avoid anything that makes them see themselves in a bad light. It is impossible for them to hang around real Christianity very long and still think as highly of themselves as they want to.

Characteristic #5: *Drifters have their roots in activities rather than in Christ.*

Teenagers can be involved in Christian activities for years before they start to drift. It's not involvement in Christian activities, however, that leads them to experience a transformed heart. The Bible teaches that the human heart is transformed only when individuals sink their roots deeply into Jesus Christ.

The Lord Jesus Christ is like no other person our kid will ever meet. Merely spending time with another human being, no matter how great that person is, won't transform a person from the inside out. But spending honest moments with Jesus Christ always will! Spending time with Him is like undergoing powerful spiritual radiation treatments that kill the cells of selfishness and pride in our hearts.

Too often, however, our teenager spends her time drinking in Christian activities, Christian friendships, even Christian teachings—but fails to ever drink in Christ Himself.

This is why a kid can be around the church for years without experiencing any real internal changes. She remains the same person, always pursuing her own goals instead of Christ's. Paul told Timothy that the goal of all Paul's teaching is love, the kind of love that can only spring from "a pure heart and a good conscience and a sincere faith" (1 Timothy 1:5).

Paul was always after people's hearts, the internal qualities which reflect that they really have a relationship with Christ. The only way to grow faith that can withstand the winds of chaos in our world is to sink our roots deep into Christ.

Characteristic #6: *Drifters are disillusioned with God's ability to deliver what they think He's supposed to deliver.*

In 1 Timothy 6:5–10 Paul warns that some pursue Christianity as a means to financial gain only later to wander away from the faith, eager for money.

In this verse Paul put his finger on the main reason drifters slip away. They drift because Christianity doesn't deliver success, popularity, money, or whatever else they originally thought it would deliver.

A kid doesn't have to be around Christianity for long to discover that God does not reward self-seeking. Ultimately, when a kid drifts away from Christianity, she does so because she does not believe God is good. Her disillusionment is with Him.

The psalmist declared that "it is *good* to be near God" (Psalm 73:28, emphasis added). The writer of Hebrews observed that "anyone who comes to [God] must believe . . . that he rewards those who earnestly seek him" (11:6).

When teenagers drift, it is because they haven't found the rewards they wanted. This explains how they can be around Christianity for years and still miss out completely on the rewards it does offer. A kid who becomes a drifter uses Christianity to seek rewards instead of God.

Christianity does provide teens with experiences of warmth, height and weight—in greater measure than they can find anywhere else in their world—but never as a reward for self-seeking, only as a reward for seeking God.

This is why it will never make sense to deserters, disputers, deceivers, dominators or defeated kids to return to Christianity until they want something more than warmth, height, and weight. Christianity will never seem like a sane or reasonable option until drifters are looking for one thing—God! The only time Christianity will not disappoint them is when they are looking for God.

The question, then, that parents of a drifter must ask is not, "How can we make Christianity attractive to our teen?" The question is, "How can we motivate our teen to seek Christ?"

How to parent a drifter

Paul wrote to Timothy about drifters for two reasons: to keep Timothy's own faith from being shaken by them, and to teach him how to help them. Paul's instructions for helping drifters are our best guidelines for dealing with our own drifting teenager.

First, deepen the root structures

According to Paul, the first thing we, as parents of a drifter, should do is sink our own roots deeper into Christ so that the winds that drew our teen away don't draw us away also. Paul told Timothy, to watch his own life and doctrine closely when he was around drifters (1 Timothy 4:16).

Parents can start to drift in what we do and what we teach if our own faith is not deeply rooted in an intimate relationship with Christ—a fixed point of stability.

On a cruise ship, when people get seasick, they are advised to fix their eyes on a stable point on the horizon. That same principle can help overcome dizziness on a merry-go-round or centrifugal-force ride.

Drifters and parents need the same thing—stable figures in our lives that we can fix our gaze on.

If we want to help our kid, we can't be drifting at the same time. When confronted with a drifting teen in our own home, it's easy for us as parents, to think, *I've trusted Christ with my child all these years and now she's walked away from Christ. What am I supposed to think about the Lord now? How can I ever trust Him again?*

When our teen, whom we care about and love, walks away from Christ, we are often tempted to let this drive a wedge between us and the Lord. That's the worst thing we can do. We need to trust God all the more because He loves our teen even more than we do.

Second, call the drifting to the drifter's attention

As we call the drifting to our teenager's attention, we can explore what's really going on. Paul told Timothy to do this in 1 Timothy 4:6. "If you point these things out to [those in your care], you will be a good minister."

In this context, Paul was talking about people who had drifted into legalism. That's as destructive as drifting into immorality. Paul instructed Timothy to point this out to them.

Whenever we see evidence of drifting in our kid, it's important to call her attention to it, but not in a way that will make her feel attacked. We need to do it in a mood of curiosity. We might say, "You know, I see some things changing in your life—things that seem to be taking you in directions that concern me. I'm not sure what it all means. Can we talk about it?"

When we encourage a drifter to tell us what disillusions her about Christianity, we will often discover that these things are not authentic Christianity at all. Exploring our teenager's disillusionment can often create opportunities to affirm her feelings.

Remember Tom, Jerry, and Matt

Tom was drifting away from Christianity because he couldn't believe that people could be Christians and be so uncaring. We found something to affirm in Tom's concerns. "You're right Tom, there are a lot of people who are just 'playing' Christian. They're not taking it seriously. The fact that it makes you sick is probably good because that's certainly not the kind of Christianity that God is calling you to. That's not His idea."

We also found something to affirm in Jerry when he chose not to go to youth group anymore. Once all the girls caught on, none of them would talk to him anymore, so he stopped coming. We told him, "You know, that's probably a good idea, Jerry. That's not what church is for—to find girls that you can take to bed with you. Let us tell you what church is really about." This opening led to a good conversation with Jerry about the essence of authentic faith in Christ.

Matt dropped out of Christianity in college because the campus ministry leadership wouldn't let him lead. In talking to him, we affirmed his decision that Christianity wasn't the place to find power over other people. "You're right, Matt, Christianity is not the route to power and influence. But if you're interested, I'll tell you where Christianity will take you."

There's almost always something to affirm in a teen's decision to drift—if we can get the kid talking about it.

Third, expose drifters to a dimension of Christianity they have never seen before

Most forms of Christianity that kids observe while growing up don't capture their imagination at all. Nothing they have seen thrills them or motivates them to give their lives to the Christian faith. Giving a kid a taste of authentic Christianity does!

Paul wrote Timothy from prison to urge him to watch the life of an unusual Christian like Onesiphorus because "he often refreshed me and was not ashamed of my chains" (2 Timothy 1:16).

Paul knew that Onesiphorus was somebody who could capture the imagination of a young man like Timothy. Capturing a teenager's imagination for Christ is one of the best ways to strengthen that kid against drifting.

Brian stopped drifting

Brian started drifting as a college freshman largely because he was unimpressed with the brand of Christianity he saw others living around him. During this time, Dick, one of the men in his church, did something that exposed Brian to a different brand of Christianity.

Instead of preaching at the skeptical teen, Dick listened to a lot of things Brian was complaining about. He said, "I understand where you're coming from. You're reacting to a Christianity that has little to do with Christ. Let me introduce you to the Christianity that you read about in the Bible. That's really what Christ is calling you to."

Then he gave Brian the book *Through Gates of Splendor,* the story of five missionaries who risked and lost their lives for Christ in the jungles of Ecuador.

It was the first time Brian had ever been exposed to anybody who loved Christ that much. These men were willing to die for Him! That made Brian think.

Next, Dick gave Brian the book *God's Smuggler,* the true story of a man who risked his life to smuggle Bibles behind what was then the Iron Curtain. Dick just kept feeding Brian books, one after the other, books that thrilled Brian and captured his imagination.

Dick did for Brian what Paul did for Timothy. He exposed him to a dimension of Christianity that made him thirsty to know Christ more deeply. That's the best thing he could have done for a drifter.

Fourth, never allow drifters to drift without experiencing the consequences

As Paul closed his final letter to Timothy, one of his last requests was for Timothy to bring Mark to him because of Mark's ability to encourage Paul.

Mark had deserted Paul on a missionary journey several years earlier, and when Mark came back to the Lord, at first Paul refused to travel with him. Later Paul wrote, "Get Mark and bring him with you because he is helpful to me in my ministry" (2 Timothy 4:11).

What a fantastic story of someone who had drifted and returned!

Perhaps it was Paul's making sure Mark experienced the consequences of drifting that helped bring Mark to his senses. Paul isolated Mark when he drifted so Mark could fully experience what it meant to be cut off from Christ.

Many times, when our kid starts to drift away from the Lord, we insulate her from the consequences. We make it seem not so bad. We cover for her. Even though she wants nothing to do with God, we make it sound as if she's all right spiritually. But drifters need honest feedback and genuine consequences.

When a drifter starts wandering away from the Lord, she misses out on so much family life in the church. This kind of isolation can be good because it helps her experience 1 Timothy 6:10 for herself: "Some people, eager for money, have wandered from the faith and pierced themselves with many griefs."

The best thing that can happen to a drifter is to be "pierced with many griefs." Many times, this is the only thing that will bring her to her senses.

As hard as this is for us as parents, we must permit our prodigal child to experience the "pig pen" of her own making. God often uses unpleasantness to create in teens a genuine desire to seek Him.

Fifth, never try to reach a drifter with pressure tactics.
In 2 Timothy 2:23 Paul gave Timothy perhaps the most important direction of all for dealing with a drifter.

> Don't have anything to do with foolish and stupid arguments, because you know they produce quarrels. . . . Instead . . . be kind, able to teach, not resentful. Those who oppose [you] gently instruct, in the hope that God will grant them repentance leading them to a knowledge of the truth, and that they'll come to their senses and escape from the trap of the devil, who has taken them captive to do his will.

Pressure tactics can never force drifting teenagers back to the Lord. Pressure usually only drives them farther away.

In these verses Paul clarifies where our responsibility as parents of a drifter ends and where God's responsibility begins. We are responsible to gently point our teen back to Christ. It's God's responsibility to give her the kind of heart that wants to follow Him.

Three

How the Enemy Calls Our Teen Away From the Faith

Nature issues so many beautiful calls to life. There's the call that sends birds on their magnificent southern migration and the call that brings monarch butterflies to their vast annual gathering in Mexico. It's the same call to life and renewal.

However, there are calls to death in nature as well. What is behind the moth's fascination with the flame, the mouse for the trap, the mosquito for the patio "zapper"? And why do the lemmings make their fatal run over the cliffs? All these creatures are answering a mesmerizing call to death.

Christ is not the only one calling our teen

Jesus issues a call to our teen. It's a call to life. But something else out there is also calling our teen. It's a tragic call to death.

Paul discussed this unseen battle in his writings to Timothy. He was concerned about keeping the enemy from harming the next generation of Christians.

The unseen war—for the hearts of our teens
In 2 Timothy 4:18 Paul describes the "evil attacks" being mounted against him, all part of a war that's being waged

against Christians and their families even today. He wrote, "The Lord will rescue me from every evil attack and will bring me safely to his heavenly kingdom."

As we guide our teen to a faith that lasts, we must become aware of this unseen battle against them and us. Often, we think our teen's problems originate only from bad communication, social pressures, or mistakes we make as parents. All of these, no doubt, contribute to teen problems, but another force—strong and destructive—is waging war against our kid.

As in any military campaign, our enemy's timeless strategy is to attack at the weakest point. Paul warned Timothy to expect the enemy to attack the weakest members of Christian families (2 Timothy 3:6).

Today, we as parents must realize that the enemy often attacks our kids during adolescence. This is a vulnerable time because our teen is declaring his independence and choosing what kind of person he wants to be. He can be easily lured away from Christ.

The invisible enemy—Satan

In 1 Timothy 5:14–15 Paul named the enemy. Here he was concerned about the enemy's attacks on the young widows in the church. "I counsel younger widows to marry, to have children, to manage their homes and to give the enemy no opportunity for slander."

Paul wanted to prevent the enemy from gaining even a toehold in our homes. He went on to say who this enemy was. "Some have in fact already turned away to follow Satan."

The words Paul used for enemy and for Satan are similar words that literally mean "adversary." Both words describe a ferocious enemy out to destroy everything God loves.

The enemy's objective—to call our teen away from God

Paul said that not only was Satan looking for any opportunity he could find to launch attacks on our families, but

Satan's real objective is to steal our family's hearts away from Christ. Paul warns, "Gently instruct, in the hope that God will grant them repentance leading them to a knowledge of the truth, and that they will come to their senses and escape from the trap of the devil, who has taken them captive to do his will" (2 Timothy 2:25–26).

Satan's objective is to take our teen captive to do his will.

The enemy's strategy—to trap our teen through intoxication
The words take captive literally mean "capture alive." In most cases, the enemy is not free to move in and hurt our kid physically. Satan has to take him as a prisoner of war—a live captive—by confusing his thinking or paralyzing his will, much like intoxication does. Satan captures our teen by putting him in a state of mind in which the road to death looks like the road to life.

A drunk driver sees the road in a different way than a sober person sees it. A drunk maneuvers his car in directions he would never go if he were not intoxicated. Once intoxicated, he'll destroy himself behind the wheel.

That's Satan's strategy with our teen, too. If he can get our kid intoxicated with something, he knows our teen will destroy himself. Satan doesn't have the power to destroy a person outright. He works on the mind to cause self-destruction. Satan wants our teen to take the road to death, thinking that it's the road to life.

Satan is glad when our kid drifts—but not satisfied. When an adolescent is drifting, there's always the chance that he may come back.

To Satan, drifting is just the first step. The second step is entrapping a teen in things that will intoxicate him. Satan knows that if he can get our teen intoxicated—get him so he's not thinking rationally—the path to death will begin to look like the path to life to him. Then he'll run right into a wall or choose from hundreds of other ways to destroy himself. And Satan loves that!

According to Paul, Satan usually uses other people to lure our kid into some activity which will be intoxicating to him. Paul writes, "The Spirit clearly says that . . . some will abandon the faith and follow deceiving spirits and things taught by demons. Such teachings come through hypocritical liars, whose consciences have been seared as with a hot iron" (1 Timothy 4:1–2).

Notice that Paul doesn't say that demons themselves seduce our kid. He says that human agents of deceit, who have gotten their ideas and messages from demonic influences, peddle their error. Paul described them as "hypocritical liars, whose consciences have been seared as with a hot iron."

Satan sends someone along to lure, seduce, coax, invite, prod, and bribe our kid into an activity that will intoxicate him. Then all the devil has to do is sit back and wait for our kid to destroy himself.

Across our country, even in Christian homes, few parents are aware of the kind of enemy we're up against or how he works. Even fewer know how to effectively combat him as he wages war against our kid.

When a nation fights a war, it doesn't matter whether the enemy is unsophisticated or sophisticated. The nation spends months preparing, gathering intelligence, and developing strategy.

The traps of the enemy

How much time do we as parents spend preparing to battle the enemy who is out to destroy our kid? Satan is so much more intelligent than any human commander. He has a larger and more sophisticated army than any nation on earth will ever be able to mobilize. His strategy for capturing our kid's heart is brilliantly sinister. Consider the traps he sets for our teen.

The fear trap

The trap Satan uses more than any other on a teenager is fear. When a person is intoxicated with fear, he doesn't think clearly.

Susan, the agoraphobic

Susan was paralyzed by possibly the most painful of all phobias—agoraphobia. Sometimes it's called the fear of open spaces or the fear of people. Essentially, however, agoraphobia is the fear of fear itself.

For Susan this fear became very destructive after she experienced a panic attack at a grocery store. The physiological symptoms were so alarming that Susan thought she was going to die. She didn't die, but the attack was so acute that Susan believed she *would* die if she experienced another one.

So Susan decided to avoid the grocery store for fear of triggering another panic attack. Eventually, Susan's "fear of fear" became so bad that she decided to never go to any grocery store again.

What was Susan afraid of? Not the grocery store. She was afraid of panic—the sensation of being out of control, helpless, paralyzed. Panic is a terrifying thing. Satan used panic to intoxicate her with fear and rob her of her ability to serve God.

Rider in the storm

Recently, I was riding my bike when a tornado came out of nowhere. The winds didn't scare me as much as the lightning cracking in the trees.

There weren't any buildings around, and I thought I was going to be hit by lightning. I panicked. I rode as hard as I could even though I could hardly see my way in the rain. Taking what I thought was the right path, I ran smack dab into a hole. My panic caused me to do something I wouldn't have done in a normal state of mind. Satan knows that fear causes a person to do things he normally wouldn't do.

Paul warned Timothy not to give in to this tactic and let fear control his actions. "For God has not given us a spirit of fear, but of power and of love and of a sound mind" (2 Timothy 1:7 NKJV).

Notice how Paul contrasted "fear" to a "sound mind." The two are opposites. Fear erodes confidence, extinguishes love, and obstructs good judgment.

That's why Satan usually resorts first to fear tactics to disable our teenager, he tries to intimidate him with threats of social ostracism or ridicule if he dares to be different around his family or friends.

I'll write you out of the will

When Tim came to Christ in high school, the enemy used Tim's father to intimidate him. Tim's dad was a very successful businessman. The last thing he wanted was a son who was a "religious fanatic."

If Tim continued in his faith, his father threatened to write him out of his will, not let him use the car, and not pay for his college tuition.

Afraid of his dad, Tim finally decided to walk away from the Lord. Satan successfully intimidated him, making the path to life look like the path to death to Tim.

Good-bye, boyfriend!

Sally, a high school junior, was afraid of losing her boyfriend. He didn't like the idea that she went to church. Every time she went, she could hardly concentrate because she was afraid he might phone her home, find out she was gone, and figure out where she was.

She tried to go about her Christian activities secretly because she didn't want to lose him. He intimidated her.

In her fear, she gradually started to abandon her faith. To Sally, keeping her boyfriend seemed like the path to life. Practicing Christianity looked like the path to death.

Satan used this intimidation strategy against Jesus' disciple Peter in the New Testament. Before the angry mob appeared, Peter was saying, "Lord, I'll never deny you. I'll stand with you to the end." However, after he saw the mob take his Lord captive, he became terrified, intimidated, intoxicated with fear.

A few hours later, when servant girls confronted him about his association with Christ, he did something he normally wouldn't do because the path to life looked like the path to death. He denied Jesus Christ.

Satan uses whatever he can to fill our kids with fear so that they'll do the same thing. Intoxication with fear is a much greater threat to our teen's health and safety than intoxication with drugs or alcohol.

Our kid is being intimidated in his high school, around his friends, and even in his own family, to do all kinds of destructive things. He doesn't like to talk about it because talking about fear tends to magnify it.

A teen can hide intoxication with alcohol and drugs for a long time, and he can hide intoxication with fear even longer. That's alarming! Often our kid falls into the fear trap without our even realizing it. But fear is only one of Satan's traps. He has many others.

The alienation trap

Satan often succeeds in intoxicating our kid with loneliness. Most of us have been deeply lonely at one time or another in our lives. During these times, it is difficult to think straight. Loneliness can be so agonizing that we will do anything to avoid feeling alone.

Paul experienced loneliness. "At my first defense, no one came to my support, but everyone deserted me" (2 Timothy 4:16).

Satan tried to silence Paul through loneliness. By making him feel alienated from other Christians, Satan was hoping Paul would crumble before Caesar and perhaps deny Christ as Peter did. This is why Paul asked Timothy to come as soon as possible. These were the words of a very lonely man.

Satan uses the same tactic on our teenager. He intoxicates a teen with the agony of loneliness. Satan wants him to feel that nobody else has the struggles or the problems he has, and that nobody understands what he's going through, so there's no use even trying to communicate his feelings to anyone—especially to adults.

Since a teen never hears adults talk about loneliness, he figures he's the only one who feels this way. That only adds to his alienation.

Juanita's plea for help

Juanita became so intoxicated with the agony of loneliness that she attempted suicide—unsuccessfully. When she woke up in the hospital and saw her family there, she was embarrassed.

"I didn't know what I was doing!" she told them. "I felt like I was drugged or something. I was so lonely I wasn't thinking straight."

Her parents were shocked, but they began to realize that Juanita had been sending them signals that she was questioning her own worth. In essence what she had been asking was, "Is there any way I can get people to love me? I feel so alone."

Juanita was reaching out, but when the alienation and loneliness didn't subside, her thinking became more and more skewed. She did something that she wouldn't have done had she been "sober."

Many kids attempt suicide because Satan has led them on an intoxicated trip down a dead-end street called loneliness. Loneliness is, perhaps, one of the hardest things for a teenager to endure. If it was hard on Paul, a grown man who knew the Lord Jesus Christ intimately, what must it be like for our kids?

The greed trap

Satan often uses materialism to intoxicate our teen with greed. Paul referred to this trap in 1 Timothy 6:9-10. "People who want to get rich fall into temptation and a trap and into many foolish and harmful desires that plunge men into ruin and destruction."

Satan knows that if he can get our teen intoxicated with greed, our kid will self-destruct.

Many high school and college students have almost destroyed their health because, in addition to school, they work almost full time to attain the material things they want. They end up with mono or burnout. There are many ways a teen can self-destruct when he becomes intoxicated with greed.

The car is boss

Ron was a very active Christian in his youth group. At sixteen he desperately wanted a car. He even prayed about it because he felt there were so many ways he could serve the Lord with a car.

Finally, his grandfather gave him one as a gift. However, Ron found out that once he had a car he had to work to pay for the gas and insurance.

The car then became a trap because he had to drop out of most of his Christian activities to earn enough money to maintain his car. Before long, instead of the car serving Ron, he was serving the car.

Satan often uses greed to rob a kid of his freedom to serve the Lord.

The immorality trap

A teen feels shame when he does something reprehensible and comes to believe he is now stained or repulsive in other people's eyes. Shame makes a teen look at himself and others differently. It becomes intoxicating. He wants to run from others and hide. He keeps to himself to avoid anyone getting to know him intimately. Shame convinces him that he could never be loved or used by God.

Jackie runs from the boys

Jackie, a heavy-set college freshman, sought help because she was doing things that she couldn't understand.

"If I'm walking down the hallway and I see a boy coming the opposite direction, I quickly turn around," she said. I can't stand to be in the same hallway with a boy. When I walk into a class that has a guy in it, I try to sit all the way on the other side of the room. If a guy comes and sits anywhere near me, I get up and leave. It is so stupid! I don't know why I'm acting that way."

With a little help from a counselor, Jackie discovered that her actions in college could be traced to an experience she had as a young teenager.

She was in her backyard one day with her older sister and a couple of her sister's male friends. For some reason, her sister went into the house and left Jackie in the backyard alone with these two boys.

The boys began to get rough with her, held her down, and took some of her clothes off, threatening to rape her. Terrified, she kicked and screamed until they let her go.

She ran into the house and hysterically reported what happened to her mom and sister. But both of them blamed her for the attack!

Her mom said, "You know that would never have happened if you didn't want those boys to do that."

Jackie didn't know what to think. Maybe her mother and sister were right. She imagined that there must be something about her appearance or personality that invited the boys to behave that way.

Jackie felt so much shame that she became intoxicated with keeping everyone at a distance. She started doing all kinds of irrational things without making conscious choices to do them.

To Jackie it looked like the path to life meant avoiding intimacy with anybody, never to be in a relationship with a man. And she must never let anybody, even women, know what kind of person she was.

To squelch her pain, Jackie began to eat constantly. Whenever she stopped eating, the shame returned. Eating was the only comfort she knew. Besides, an obese figure deterred people from trying to get close to her.

Shame is beneath a lot of eating disorders. And Satan often uses sexual experiences, as he did with Jackie, to keep kids intoxicated with shame and convinced of their unworthiness.

The body trap

Paul warned Timothy of this trap in 1 Timothy 4:7, "Have nothing to do with godless myths and old wives' tales."

There were some myths going around at that time, promising immortality and eternal bliss to those who could attain a perfect physique. Greek society was obsessed with bodybuilding. That's why Paul went on to say, "rather, train yourself to be godly. For physical training is of some value, but godliness has value for . . . the life to come."

Today, Satan tries to get our teen obsessed with physical fitness and appearance. When our kid becomes convinced that some deficiency in his body is blocking the path to life, correcting this deficiency becomes an obsession. Our kid becomes intoxicated with the quest for the impossible; bodies that can capture all the acclaim, attention, and affection he craves.

James the jogger

James started running a couple of miles a day when he was fifteen. By the time he was seventeen, he felt guilty if he didn't run at least a hundred miles every week.

He was obsessed. Running was all he ever thought about. When he was sitting in church, he was trying to figure out how to get his miles in that day. He planned his meals, his day, his whole existence around running. There was no time to think about relationships or other important matters. Satan had him where he was absolutely useless to anybody for anything.

Other kids may be obsessed with weight, hair, or percentage of body fat. Whatever it is, it's intoxicating, and it leads them into self-destructive and self-absorbed lifestyles.

The legalism trap

Paul warned Timothy about the legalists in 1 Timothy 4:3–4. "They forbid people to marry and order them to abstain from certain foods." Legalists claim that life depends on following more and more rules.

Rulekeeping can also be intoxicating. Remember the Pharisees? They were intoxicated with self-righteousness and pride, a state of mind that obstructed any kind of genuine relationship with Christ or anybody else.

A new Christian is quite susceptible to this trap. Shortly after coming to Christ, a teen often begins to add all kinds of laws and rules to his Christian faith. He can get so intoxicated with the sense of moral superiority that rulekeeping gives that he can't even talk casually with others about everyday events. It's like trying to get a drunk into a rational conversation.

A person intoxicated with pride and self-righteousness can't talk like a normal person.

Jeff, the spiritual giant

Jeff went on a missions trip with his youth group. At the wrap-up meeting when they returned home, several of the teens mentioned what a great spiritual leader Jeff was on the trip.

For the first time Jeff felt like a somebody. He realized that if he could just keep people praising him for being a spiritual leader, he could maintain this feeling.

So Jeff started fasting two or three days a week. One day, while trying to impress someone, he said, "I don't know how anybody who doesn't fast could really know the Lord."

Next, he decided that Sunday was the Lord's day, and no one should be going to restaurants, working, purchasing gas, or shopping on Sundays because it made people "violate the Sabbath."

Later, he added another rule to his life. He decided he needed at least two hours a day to read his Bible. And he let everybody in the youth group know that he got up every morning before dawn to read the Bible and pray. The energy behind all of Jeff's attempts to be "spiritual" came from his desire to keep the praise coming.

When Jeff experienced praise for his spiritual leadership on the missions trip, it became intoxicating. But he paid a price for it. He lost his capacity to be a real spiritual encourager to others. Satan had him right where he wanted him.

The bitterness trap

Satan often gets a teenager so angry that the kid does and says things he would never say in his right mind. That's what it's like to be intoxicated with anger. This is the trap Pete fell into.

Was Pete offsides?

Every Sunday evening before Bible study, all the men of the church would meet in the parking lot for a game of touch football. It was a great time for the high school and college kids to mix with the men in the church.

The first time Pete came out to play, the pastor accused him of cheating. He said that Pete moved before the ball was hiked. Insulted, Pete left immediately. He was so angry that he felt justified in getting drunk with his fraternity brothers that night.

The next morning, the anger was still there. Pete was intoxicated with anger, which grew into bitterness. He had fallen right into Satan's trap. Pete wasn't thinking right. He almost left the church permanently.

A number of men from the church, including the pastor himself, had to come and talk to Pete before the anger started to diffuse.

Satan knows how to lead a teen into the bitterness trap. All he has to do is put the teen in a situation in which another Christian hurts him and angers him. Over time, when the anger is not shared or talked about, it grows and begins to affect the teenager's whole outlook on life. That's why, in 1 Timothy 5:1–2, Paul warns us not to give Satan an opportunity to embitter us in the way we talk to each other in the church. He says, "Do not rebuke an older man harshly, but exhort him as if he were your father. Treat younger men as brothers, older women as mothers, and younger women as sisters, with absolute purity."

The idleness trap

Paul warned Timothy that young widows in the church were especially vulnerable to this trap. "They get into the habit of being idle and going about from house to house. And not only do they become idlers, but also gossips and busybodies, saying things they ought not to" (1 Timothy 5:13).

Idleness creates boredom. And studies on teenage stress show that boredom is always in the top five causes of teenage depression and misbehavior.

When a teenager becomes bored, underchallenged, or inactive, he begins to think about doing things he would never consider otherwise. This often happens when a family uproots a teen from his friends and activities, and moves to an area where he has nothing to keep himself occupied. Intoxicated with boredom, a teen may do things he never considered before.

Boredom gets to Megan

Megan was a very strong, committed Christian. Although she had many opportunities at school to party and become involved in illicit activities, Megan wasn't interested. She never even considered it.

Then the summer after her junior year of high school, her family moved. Megan didn't know anybody in her new school, and she thought the kids were snobbish. Without even a church youth group around to get involved in, she grew bored and restless.

Out of desperation, she got a job. At work, she met a bunch of new kids. They invited her to a party— the kind she had said no to a hundred times before. But, because she was intoxicated with boredom, she wasn't thinking clearly.

She started to accept their invitations and go behind her parents' backs, doing things she never would have done just a few months previously. She was caught in the idleness trap.

Signs that show a teen is trapped

Since the traps that our teenager could fall into are so numerous and dangerous, it is important that we as parents quickly recognize when our teen falls into one of them. There are several clear warning signs to watch for.

Loss of passion

The first sign that a teen has become "entrapped" is a loss of passion for the things he normally loves (the Lord, his family, his friends). His passion will be transferred to new interests, things that rob him of any sense of aliveness or vitality.

We can see it in his eyes first. Confusion. Exhaustion. Coldness. Paul warned that once a person starts living for pleasure, "[he's] dead even while [he] lives" (1 Timothy 5:6). When we look into the eyes of someone who's intoxicated, we can always see it. We know that something's wrong. His passion for everything that's good disappears.

Loss of Interest

The next telltale sign will be a loss of interest in all his normal, routine responsibilities. They will seem unimportant in comparison to whatever intoxicates him. Nothing will matter to him as much as what promises him relief from fear, shame, anger, or boredom.

Loss of respect

Another sign will be a loss of respect for authority. Just as someone who is drunk loses respect for traffic signals, a kid who is caught in one of Satan's traps will lose respect for anyone who tries to direct him away from the path he has chosen.

Ineffective strategies we use

Once intoxicated, a teenager will inevitably fall into self-destructive behaviors. When we start to see these behaviors, we must be careful not to respond in ways that only further intoxicate the teen.

Emotional blackmail

Many parents try to control an intoxicated teenager by emphasizing how much he is hurting them. They try to make the teen feel guilty enough to cease the behavior. However, emotional blackmail is just another form of intimidation, which only adds to a teenager's fear and shame.

Change of environment

Other parents may think that getting their teenager into a new high school or youth group is the answer.

Changing a teen's environment, however, often results in taking his friends and support network from him, which only adds to his alienation and loneliness. Chances are, at the new school our teen will act even more irrational and self-destructive because his pain has increased.

Bribes

Some parents may say, "If you behave, I'll buy you new clothes, a stereo or even a car." But, bribery only intoxicates our teen more with pride and greed. It's like using alcohol to bribe a drunk. "Listen, I'll give you this bottle of whiskey if you'll stop drinking." That's what we're doing when we bribe our teen with possessions, trips, or other material possessions, in exchange for good behavior.

Emotional experiences with the Lord

Others think the answer is to send the teen away to a Christian camp or retreat. We try to schedule enough mountaintop experiences to keep him on a perpetual "spiritual high."

But this only makes a teenager dependent on sensational experiences. He becomes addicted to the rush. When the church retreat fails to get him pumped anymore, he begins to look for something else that will give him a high.

Arguing

Some of us try arguing our teen sober. However, this strategy only adds to his bitterness and intoxicates him more with anger. Paul warned Timothy not to quarrel with people who have been caught in Satan's traps.

Rules

How about rules? What effect do more rules have on an intoxicated teenager? If he keeps them, rules could make him a legalist and intoxicate him even more with pride. But, intoxicated teens usually ignore rules anyway.

Strategies that will work

So, if the above strategies won't work, what will? The good news is there are two strategies we can use to effectively fight the war Satan is waging against our teenager.

Spiritual warfare requires being at REST with our teen

The REST strategy[*] calls for implementing four principles into our parenting:

R — Reflection
E — Exploration
S — Surrender
T — Teaching

Reflection. Before responding to problems in our teen's life, we must first reflect on our own hearts.

---

*For a more complete discussion of the REST strategy see Kevin Huggins and Phil Landrum, *Making Peace With Your Teenager* (Grand Rapids: Discovery House Publishers, 1993), 143–204.

Do we have an agenda of our own that takes precedence over what's best for our teen? Are we more concerned with how his actions will make us look? Or, are we motivated by a deeper commitment to guide him to a faith that lasts?

Being at REST starts by reflecting on our own agenda as parents and making sure it is the same as Christ's. Aligning our agenda with Christ's frees us to selflessly fight for our teen.

Exploration. When we actively explore the pressures in our teen's world and heart that take him away from Christ, we can detect where and how the enemy is attacking him. Our awareness also communicates to our teenager that he is not alone in this battle. He has a strong ally in his parents.

Surrender. After reflecting on ourselves and exploring our teen, surrender is our only option. We can never defeat Satan if we're fighting God at the same time.

Spiritual victory in our family begins with surrendering our hearts and our adolescent to Christ—calling on Him to do for us and our teen what we could never do for ourselves. He can give us the kind of hearts that can never be lured away from Him!

Teaching. Surrender takes off the pressure to be perfect parents or raise the perfect teen. It puts the pressure back on God's shoulders, where it belongs, and frees us to teach our kid from a position of rest instead of desperation. Pressure always hurts our relationship with our teen and blocks or distorts the messages we're trying to send him about God. Reflection, exploration, and surrender provide a game plan for what and how we teach our teenager.

Spiritual warfare requires us to use the principles of warfare against the enemy

The Bible teaches that we are at war with the evil forces of this world. Very intelligent and powerful, these evil forces make the world a hostile and frightening place to parent a teenager. This is why Christian parents must go on the offense and resist the enemy, who wants to capture the hearts and minds of our kids.

The apostle Paul instructed Timothy to take the offense by following tried and true principles of war. These are the same principles successful and military commanders have followed for centuries.

We parents can easily apply these principles to the spiritual battles we face with our teen.

The principle of objective

When we see our teenager being attacked by Satan, we must respond with a clear objective in mind. Throughout 1 and 2 Timothy, Paul kept coming back to what our objective should be: "Keep giving them the truth."

Truth is the only thing that will cut through our teenager's fog and confusion. Mere human words will not get through. When we speak the truth of God, the Spirit of God uses it to bring our teen to his senses.

This doesn't necessarily mean to quote the Bible to the kid all the time. But it does mean to pass on biblical truth—*mostly through the messages we send with our lives.* Paul's reminder to Timothy is true today: when people are caught up in the trap of the devil, they need gentle instruction.

The false messages our teen has been receiving are intoxicating. Truth is the only thing that doesn't further intoxicate. For many years the standard treatment for sobering a drunk has been to make him drink coffee. The only thing that sobers our kid when he's intoxicated with Satan's lies is truth—God's truth, gently spoken and quietly lived out in front of him in a spirit of love. That's our primary objective when waging spiritual war: to keep speaking the truth in love to our teen.

The principle of concentration

The enemy of Christians expects to find the weakest defenses around our teenager. Often, he can get near a teenager and lure him into intoxicating activities with little or no resistance.

Before this happens, we must deploy our forces where the enemy least expects them. Around every teen, we need to concentrate *a team of caring Christians, praying and spending time with him.*

It's especially critical to concentrate our forces at the first appearance of any sign of intoxication or drifting. If we do, often we'll see our teen spared or rescued from many destructive experiences.

Paul knew how important this principle was. When he felt abandoned and attacked, he asked his Christian friends to concentrate on him. He was saying, in essence, I've been left all alone. Although Luke is with me, that's not enough. Would you make sure that Mark comes. I need people around me. I'm being attacked right now and I need you to concentrate forces to help me out.

We would be wise to follow Paul's example even earlier. Before we sense Satan's attack, we need to ask other Christians to concentrate their prayers on our families. The enemy is too powerful for any of us to face alone.

The principle of cooperation

We must continually remind ourselves that *our teenager is not the enemy,* nor is he the only one in our home who has spiritual struggles. We are prone to drift and fall into Satan's traps as much as our teen is. We all need help from other Christians to resist the enemy's attacks.

This cooperation is vital! As parents, we must coordinate our efforts with the church's youth and family ministries. During wartime, we cannot afford the luxury of fighting among ourselves or working alone. Youth workers need our help. As parents, we need the youth workers' help. And our kid needs both!

Jesus observed that a house divided falls. So does a church. Too often, the Christians in our teenager's life don't have any idea what the others are trying to do. Sometimes, out of ignorance, jealousy, or suspicion, they work against each other. As a result, youth workers and parents become critical of each other and fail to take advantage of the wealth of resources and knowledge the other has.

Parents or youth workers who ignore the principle of cooperation limit the amount of spiritual help a teen gets. Those who pray and work together multiply the impact each has with a teen.

The principle of communication

Paul knew that successful warfare requires keeping all his allies informed.

Paul warned Timothy to watch out for the activities of Alexander the metal worker. Then he added, "Do your best to come to me quickly, for Demas, because he loved this world, has deserted me and has gone to Thessalonica. Crescens has gone to Galatia, and Titus to Dalmatia. . . . I sent Tychicus to Ephesus" (2 Timothy 4:9–15).

All through his letters, Paul informed fellow Christians what their enemies and allies were doing. *He also let them know what his own needs were and how they could help him.*

As parents, we follow this principle when we let other Christians know that our teenager is struggling. If there were more communication among us when our teens have spiritual troubles, we could muster greater spiritual support on his behalf and better resist the enemy.

Too often, however, Satan convinces us not to talk to each other about our family struggles. It's too embarrassing!

Then Satan has us exactly where he wants us—isolated, struggling and fighting our spiritual battles alone.

The principle of supply

This war tactic reminds us to never allow a break in our supply routes. Paul said that no one defended him when Alexander caused trouble, "but the Lord stood at my side and gave me strength" (2 Timothy 4:16–17).

Paul remained strong because his supply lines were never broken. He looked to both fellow Christians and the Lord for the supplies he needed for spiritual warfare. Even when his church friends failed him, he could always find support from the Lord.

Too often, when things start to go wrong at home, we cut our own supply lines out of anger or embarrassment. We stop talking to people at church. We even stop talking to God!

That's what Satan wants. He wants us to be cut off from our reinforcements. The principle of supply teaches us that *victory cannot be accomplished without resupply and reinforcements.* That's why God always finds a way to provide both for those who fight for Him.

The key for us as Christian parents is to keep our supply lines intact at all times, especially when the odds seem overwhelming. Our relationship with Christ and fellow Christians must be maintained at all costs.

The principle of offense

When the enemy is trying to attack us, we should mount a counterattack in his own territory.

Perhaps a parent's best defense against Satan's assaults on our teenager is to seek to reach his friends for Christ.

Every church or group of Christian parents should have an active plan for reaching the unsaved high school kids in their community.

Every time we invade the enemy's territory and lead an unsaved high school student to Christ, we weaken Satan's ability to attack our teen. When our teen starts seeing spiritual victories in his peers' lives, he will be greatly encouraged in his own faith. A strong counteroffensive sends the enemy on the run.

The principle of mobility

Christian parents and youth workers in the church are wise to anticipate where Satan might strike and get there first.

If the church has a teen retreat scheduled for this weekend, it's safe to assume that Satan will be doing all he can to prevent anything good from happening there. Everything that could go wrong probably will unless a team of caring adults anticipates his opposition and strikes first. What if a group of us went there early and prayed our hearts out for the whole weekend?

Or, what if we anticipate how Satan might be attacking a certain teenager? If a Christian teen is elected as president of the student body at school or makes the football or cheerleading squad, we ought to assemble a team to pray specifically for that kid. We can anticipate that a Christian teen in a high-profile position will be a major target of the enemy. Paul repeatedly warned Timothy to anticipate the enemy's attacks and strike first to deny Satan an opening.

The principle of pursuit

This principle calls for us to follow up every small victory with an offensive of our own. Whenever we see spiritual breakthroughs in our kid, it's time to focus our resources on nurturing and encouraging him.

If we see a teenager who has been intoxicated with anger finally begin to soften, it's important to remember that the battle isn't over yet. The principle of pursuit calls for getting him into a discipleship group. Team him up with an adult or peer encourager to meet on a regular basis.

Continue to assemble a team of Christians to pray for him. Let's not settle for just having him back at church. Too often we stop our offensive after winning small skirmishes in our teen's life. As a result, we miss the opportunity to see his whole heart taken captive by Christ.

When we parents wage war using these principles, we will see breakthroughs in our family unlike anything we could imagine. God is ready to start! We must be ready to let Him!

He is able to do more than all we ask or imagine, according to His power that is at work within us! (Ephesians 3:20).

Being at REST with our teen but at war with the evil forces in his world is key to effectively calling our teen to a faith that lasts.

Four

How Faith Takes Hold and
Grows in Our Teen

A building doesn't just happen. Through a logical construction process, it develops from a mere image in an architect's mind into a completed, furnished structure. The process involves many stages of precise and painstaking labor—specified by a master blueprint or model.

Our teenager's faith develops the same way.

As parents, we have our own model for faith development which determines what kind of spiritual nurture we give our teen. However, faulty models can misguide us or result in actions that are actually destructive to our teen's faith.

Faulty models for building faith

The heritage model

Some parents operate from a model which presents faith as something a kid *inherits* or *acquires* by being part of a religious family or a church. Like ethnic heritage, faith is something their kids have grown up with.

Parents (and churches) using this model usually measure faith by the degree to which a person practices the traditions and attends the services of her faith. Spiritual nurture, according to this model, usually involves little more than requiring a teenager to participate in these practices.

While it's not difficult to keep a child actively participating in a faith that she has basically "inherited" from her family, a teenager feels little internal compulsion to keep religious traditions that seem unrelated to her primary pursuits in life.

The confirmation model

This model presents faith as something a young person qualifies for by acquiring religious knowledge and skills usually during early adolescence. Once she does this, she is "confirmed" in the faith or recognized to be a person of faith.

In this model, spiritual nurture usually consists of rote learning and recitation with the promise of both immediate and eternal rewards when the task is completed.

Although a kid nurtured in a family that holds to this model demonstrates some tendency to keep practicing the faith she was raised in, she may have difficulty integrating her religious faith with her daily life, especially when severe trials occur.

The faith-event model

According to this model, faith is something "caught" rather than "taught." It occurs in a moment of crisis or emotion when a young person realizes her need for God and makes a commitment to follow Him.

When we follow this model, we attempt to spiritually nurture our teen by providing a series of emotional experiences that lead her to deeper and deeper commitments to God and eventually to the state of "being totally sold out to Him."

This often involves taking our teen to events where she can have "mountaintop experiences"—camps, youth rallies, or Christian concerts.

Although this form of spiritual nurture does temporarily elicit great enthusiasm and radical changes in a teen, it usually cannot sustain this condition beyond a few months or a few years.

The faith-event model also pressures us to keep subjecting our teen to more and more sensational "spiritual challenges." Seldom, however, does the spiritual fervor ignited by these faith events last after the sensational challenges stop.

Sensationalism addicts the adolescent to emotional spiritual experiences. After the event is over, the fire fizzles.

The biblical model—faith building

Each of these models has little in common with the model Paul used to nurture Timothy's faith. Paul's model might best be described as a *faith-building model*. This model views faith as something that gradually develops in a young person's life as she becomes personally persuaded that God is someone she can trust and love.

According to Paul, faith is a matter of personal conviction. The word *faith* comes from a Greek word that means "to be persuaded." It refers to a personal conviction that begins as a seed planted in a heart and slowly grows from a tender shoot into a mighty oak.

What faith building isn't . . .

Faith building isn't a result of pressure. Pressure is the enemy of faith. It obstructs the growth of true faith. The cradle of genuine faith is personal inquiry, reflection, and experience. Nothing else can send the roots of a teenager's soul deeper and deeper, searching for meaningful satisfaction, ultimately leading her to God. Pressure only impedes this process.

Faith building isn't accidental. Nurturing genuine faith in a teen is time-intensive. It requires great gentleness, patience, and faithfulness from the teen's parents.

Faith building isn't a temporary fix. It is the only type of spiritual nurture that can help a teen develop a permanent root structure for a faith that lasts a lifetime.

Faith building isn't the result of controlling our teen's environment. As Christian parents, it's easy to assume that we can strengthen our teenager's faith if we subject her to enough Christian rules, insist on near-constant adult supervision, and surround her with as many other Christians as possible. However, genuine faith can never be imposed externally on others.

Faith building isn't the result of forced love. By definition, Christian convictions must flow from voluntary love, not forced love. When Christianity is forced on a teenager, she might maintain a surface commitment to Christianity simply because she's afraid to outwardly resist. However, without personal choice, her roots of faith can't go very deep. Teens usually abandon an imposed faith as soon as the pressure is removed.

What faith building is

Faith building involves a conviction about something invisible. Our teen must personally become persuaded of something that concrete evidence and scientific fact cannot generate. She must take a leap in the dark, choosing to entrust to God all that she holds precious, even though she can't physically see, taste, touch, or hear Him. She must trust this invisible authority with her life over and above any number of visible authorities she could trust instead.

Faith building involves freedom of choice. It's a scary thing for us as parents to communicate to our teenager that, when it comes to faith, this is a choice only our teen can make. Although it's scary, our acceptance of this fact is essential to our teenager's faith development.

How faith building develops

Paul described Timothy's faith building as a process of personal "persuasion." Timothy had to be convinced in his own heart about Jesus Christ. Not a one-time event, Timothy's faith building was a series of events or experiences through which he slowly became persuaded that this was what he wanted.

Faith building is a process that takes time

In 2 Timothy 3:14 Paul describes the way Timothy's faith progressed. "As for you, continue in what you have learned and have become convinced of."

First, Timothy learned about Christ from others. Later, after evaluating and experiencing the truths he heard, he became personally convinced that what he learned was true.

It's important for us to remember that it takes time for genuine faith to develop. We need to show our kids the same kind of patience Paul showed Timothy.

Faith building is a process that involves active participation

Although Timothy grew immensely in his spiritual development through input from his mother, grandmother, and Paul, the biblical language in 1 and 2 Timothy depicts this young man as an active agent in the process—not a passive one. Faith can never be developed in a person's heart without that person being an active participant in the process.

Passively, our teens learn a lot about Christianity in Sunday school and at home as they are growing up. However, they will remain unconvinced and uncommitted to what they learned until they actively question, weigh, and test those beliefs for themselves. Often, this doesn't begin until adolescence.

Art goes on a binge

Art became a Christian in high school. During this time, he learned a lot about God's grace and forgiveness. However, because he was a pretty good kid, Art wasn't aware of being very sinful.

So, when he heard about Christ cleansing wicked hearts, it seemed abstract. This concept had not become a conviction because he had no personal experience with God's grace. He didn't know he needed it.

In his first year of college Art became discouraged when he ran into opposition to his efforts to win his whole campus for Christ. He got so discouraged that, on his eighteenth birthday, he went out and got "wild drunk." This was the first time he had ever drunk alcohol. When he came back to the dorm and staggered down the halls, the guys Art had been witnessing to for three months were astounded.

Art's roommate wasn't around when Art returned, so some of the other guys put him to bed in the top bunk. Art's roommate had no inkling about this drunken binge until, in the middle of the night, Art rolled over in his sleep and threw up all over his roommate. Art didn't even wake up.

It took a few days before the roommate would even talk to him to tell him what had happened. Then, Art felt ashamed. He felt he had disgraced Christ's name and blown any chance that the guys in his dorm would ever find Christ. He thought God would never forgive him.

In the days and weeks that followed, Art found out that Christ was compassionate to forgive him, and also work in the lives of the other students in that dorm despite his actions. Before the semester ended, God allowed Art to lead his roommate and several other students in the dorm to Christ.

Without this experience Art would never have become personally convinced of how full of grace Christ really is! Personal persuasion sank the roots of Art's faith far deeper than any amount of preaching or pressure from others ever could have done.

Faith building is a process in which the outcome is not certain

In 2 Timothy 1, Paul described this process as one in which a living faith is carefully nurtured in a young person like a small flame or a tender plant. Paul said, "I have been reminded of your sincere faith, which first lived in your grandmother Lois and your mother Eunice and, I am persuaded, now lives in you also" (v. 5).

Note that Paul himself also had to be persuaded, over time, that Timothy's faith was sincere and would last.

If we're honest, we have to admit we're not yet convinced what our teenager will ultimately do with her faith in Christ. We know how fickle her heart can be because we know how fickle our own hearts are.

Although others may be persuaded that our teenager will be the next Billy Graham, it takes a lot more to convince us. We live with our teen.

This is why Paul went on to tell his son in the faith, "I remind you to fan into flame the gift of God, which is in you through the laying on of my hands" (2 Timothy 1:6). Paul knew that Timothy's faith was still a relatively small flame that must be tended or it could go out.

Remember the parable of the four soils in Matthew 13? In two cases, there was some growth at first, but because of adverse conditions, spiritual growth soon withered and died. In the same way, faith in a young person is fragile. Unless our teenagers nurture their own tender plant of faith, it could die.

Faith building is a process that exposes the true nature of our teen's faith

Not until Paul witnessed Timothy's faith surviving and growing in spite of adversity did he become convinced that the young man's faith was sincere.

The word *sincere* is an interesting one. It means "without wax."

In Paul's day freelance sculptors would travel from town to town and offer, for a fee, to sculpt a statue of the town's favorite god or hero. As they labored over the expensive block of marble or granite provided by the town, there was little room for error—especially with the delicate facial features.

Often, however, these not-so-skilled sculptors would, in one wrong chisel blow, inadvertently chip the nose or ear off. Too frightened or embarrassed to go back to the town and tell the officials they needed to start over with a new block of stone, they would color some wax to match the stone and then shape the facial feature out of it.

After finishing, they would quickly collect payment and get out of town before the statue could be moved outdoors. As soon as the statue was unveiled, the sun would melt the wax and expose the artists' "insincerity."

Paul didn't want Timothy's faith to melt under heat. As Timothy's spiritual father, Paul was after a faith that lasts. That kind of faith couldn't be rushed or "glued on." It had to slowly grow within as Timothy came to the same conclusion about Jesus Christ that his mother and grandmother came to years earlier.

The same is true today. Before we can be sure that a living faith has taken root in our teens, they must go through a series of faith-growing experiences and conclude on their own that Jesus Christ is worth serving.

Ken's disappointing Bible study

Ken was a real go-getter after he became a Christian in high school. Before long the youth pastor asked Ken to lead a Bible study on the subject of disappointment.

During the Bible study, Ken emphasized the fact that God uses disappointment to make Christians stronger, more dependent on Him. But Ken was teaching from knowledge, not experience. At church he had learned how Christians are supposed to handle disappointment, but he hadn't yet had an opportunity to personally test what he had learned.

While Ken was teaching, the youth pastor took a telephone message for Ken, but waited to give it to him until the Bible study was over. Then, he called Ken away from the group.

"Ken, that was the district Christian education office on the phone," the youth pastor told him. "You know last week they told you that you'd won the top scholarship for the writing contest? Well, it turned out they miscounted. You got second instead."

For the first time as a Christian, Ken discovered what he really believed about disappointment. At first, he wasn't persuaded that this was for his own good. "This is a rip-off," he blurted out. "It isn't fair. How can God possibly let this happen?"

Moments before, Ken had been teaching that God uses disappointment for our good. However, when faced with reality, he concluded that if God was going to let this kind of stuff happen, he wasn't sure he wanted to serve Him.

It took several days of prayer, reflection, and inquiry for Ken to be persuaded that what he was teaching the other kids about God was right. God allowed disappointment in his life for a good reason. On his own, Ken discovered that he could trust God in the middle of disappointment. No one could have forced this conviction on him. And reaching this conclusion on his own deepened Ken's faith.

Faith building is a process that leads our teen into firsthand encounters with Jesus Christ.

In 2 Timothy 1:12 Paul described to Timothy what was the foundation of his own faith. "I am not ashamed, because I know whom I have believed, and am convinced that he is able to guard what I have entrusted to him for that day."

Paul was putting his faith in someone he knew personally. He had frequently encountered Jesus Christ in his own life. That's why Paul had confidence that if Timothy had his own personal encounters with Jesus Christ, he too would become persuaded to serve Him for a lifetime.

The only thing that persuades teenagers not to live for themselves is a personal encounter with the Lord Jesus Christ that wrestles the adolescent spirit into joyful obedience.

High school rumble in the making

Greg, a new Christian, was a fast-track kid. Although only a senior in high school, he had been promoted to building supervisor at the local YMCA four nights a week.

One day at school, a crowd of guys came up to him. "Listen, Greg," one of them said, "we know you're in charge of the 'Y,' so we're coming over there tonight for a rumble. We're going to use the big room over there because none of us want to get arrested for fighting on the street. You let us in and don't tell anybody."

Greg stammered around and tried to talk them out of it, but they insisted.

Greg was stumped. Should he neglect his responsibilities as supervisor of the building and let them do it? Should he tell the executive director at the YMCA and risk getting the guys in trouble? They might all come after him!

As a new Christian, Greg's quandary was his first big test of faith. He decided to leave school early. All he knew to do was to sit in his car and pray. That afternoon, Greg had an encounter with Christ in his car that he'll never forget!

The Lord assured Greg that he could trust Him. Greg sensed that God wanted him to tell the YMCA executive director about the rumble. So, he did.

He imagined the director would call the police, but instead, the director went out and rented a bunch of boxing gloves and got refreshments. When the guys arrived that night, they put on the gloves and had an organized rumble, complete with referees. The kids loved it.

Greg came out of that experience more convinced than ever that Jesus Christ would never fail him—all because of the personal encounter he had with God.

As parents, we must forget the idea that we can make our kids into spiritual giants if we just do enough for them. Real faith only takes root and spreads through a teen's own personal encounters with Christ.

Seven stages of faith building

We can expect teens to pass through seven stages in their spiritual development. In his letter to Timothy, Paul alludes to these stages, and if we, as parents, learn to recognize them, they can be a strategic tool in understanding and encouraging our teen's faith development.

A word of warning: *Expect a lot of challenges, questions, and even disbelief from your teen as she progresses through these seven stages.*

If we want to be the spiritual guide our teen needs most, we will encourage personal inquiry and reflection. In order for our teen's faith to grow, she must ask some hard questions at every stage of her faith development. At least one major question must be answered at each stage in order for a teenager to progress to the next stage. If a teen stops asking questions and searching for answers, faith development will not only stop; it will start to reverse.

Normally, growth through these stages is gradual and sequential. When a teen appears to jump stages, it is usually temporary at best. Sooner or later, she will return to the stages she skipped to do the foundational work of inquiry and reflection she missed.

That's all right.

This prevents her from building a house before the foundation is in place. A house without a foundation will not withstand the storms of life.

This is why God grows faith much like He grows fruit on a tree. Faith never arrives fully developed. It begins small and immature and grows in stages. First the roots. Then the trunk and branches. And finally the fruit itself. It is vital that parents recognize and encourage faith at each stage and in all its immature forms.

Stage 1: *Hearing about a God the teen doesn't know*

The Bible declares that faith comes by hearing and hearing by the word of God (Romans 10:17). Paul kept reminding Timothy "to let what you've heard from me" be the foundation of his faith. This is the stage at which every teenager begins a personal journey of faith: listening to God's truths from the Bible.

Teen's question: Why should I listen?

When a teen is first exposed to the teachings of the Bible, she must wrestle with the question, "Is this something that deserves my attention?"

Seldom does a teenager ask this question aloud. So, we don't often have the opportunity to answer her directly. Nevertheless, a kid must ask it in her heart if the seeds of faith are ever to start sprouting within.

Parent's response: Passion.

The best way we parents can convince our teen that the Bible does deserve her attention is to expose her to people who follow the truths of the Bible with real passion. Teenagers listen the most to those who speak with passion about what they believe. When kids hear parents or other adults in the church talking about Christianity with no sense of passion, they pay little attention.

What gets the attention of teenagers more than anything else? Hearing somebody (who seems to be like them) speaking passionately about Christ. That's when they stop and listen. Too often, teenagers write off Christianity because they see it as an "adult thing"—not something for young people like them.

This is why we'll never get our teen thinking seriously about Christianity until we start to speak honestly to her about our own struggles and about how Christ helps us in the midst of them. This is what gives our words passion. A teen knows when adults are pretending. Insincerity is the quickest turn-off for an adolescent.

When a teenager finally decides, "Yes, the teachings of the Bible really do deserve my attention," she moves to the second stage in her faith development.

Stage 2: *Flirting with a God the teen may want*

Paul pictured people at this stage—flirting with Christianity—much like a fish flirts with a piece of bait before swallowing it. In 1 Timothy 6:5 Paul described people who toyed with Christianity because they thought godliness was a means to great gain. While flirting, they tried to figure out what faith in Christ offered them.

Teen's question: What's in it for me?

When a teenager begins to flirt with Christianity, she asks, "Is this something that offers me what I'm looking for? Will I like it?"

Parent's response: It all depends.

We must be very careful how we help our teenager answer this question. Our teen may be looking for success, revenge, a way to feel powerful. Christianity is not a good means to achieve those things. It is wise to answer, "It all depends. What are you looking for?"

This question helps our teen take a hard look at herself, asking, "What am I looking for? What do I want?"

When we see our teenager starting to flirt with the Christian faith, we need to be alert. Maybe she just came back from a concert where she heard a band member talking passionately about Jesus Christ, and by her own choice she begins to attend a campus Bible study. At this point we could say, "Hey, I've noticed that you've been attending Bible study the past few weeks. What's going on?"

"Well, I don't know. Some things I've been hearing about God lately really have me thinking."

"Would you like to talk about them?"

As we have opportunity, it's important to clarify for our teen what Christianity does and does not offer. Encouraging our teen to pursue Christianity for self-aggrandizing purposes only backfires in the long run. Ultimately, she'll become disillusioned with Christ and drift away from Him when God fails to massage her ego.

Christianity offers a whole different path to life for the teen who has become disillusioned with the path of self-aggrandizement. Faith in Christ offers life—life which results from the death of self-centeredness. It is only fair to make this clear to anyone who flirts with Christianity.

Having decided that Christ does offer what she wants out of life, our teen enters another faith-development stage. She becomes a serious student of Christianity.

Stage 3: *Studying about a God who puzzles the teen*

Any teenager who comes near genuine Christianity soon discovers that the God of the Bible is like no one she's ever encountered before. God operates by no one else's rules or reason. He has His own plans for the world, and these plans involve everybody and everything. His ways are so confounding that they must be studied to be believed.

This is why a teenager will never be able to give her whole heart to Christ until she first has an opportunity to study God's ways.

Teen's question: What will happen?

During this stage, a teen begins to ask, "What will happen to me if I turn my life over to this person who behaves like no one I've ever known? What will my life be like?"

Parent's response: Provide safe places to study.

It's important for us as parents to remember that when our teen begins to study Christianity, it doesn't necessarily mean she's making a commitment.

It's important that we provide our teen a safe environment in which she can come and study the Bible, ask questions, and express doubts without pressure for commitments.

Often, a kid moves out of Stage 3 too quickly because someone finds out about her interest in Christianity and pressures her to make a commitment she's not ready to make yet. This cuts short opportunity for honest study and leads to shallow or aborted spirituality.

This is why it is so destructive for church youth workers to give teenagers the message that only committed people are welcome around church youth groups. Some youth pastors have this philosophy: I don't have much time, so I'm only going to work with the committed kids.

Too often, the kids that these youth workers identify as "committed" are the kids who have never gone through the stages of faith development and are feigning a commitment imposed on them by the adults in their world.

Perhaps the high school kid who is closer to true commitment is the one who is asking questions, expressing doubts, and struggling openly with her confusion about God.

We must provide environments in our homes and churches where teens like this can openly ask questions without being treated like there is something wrong with them.

Why shouldn't a teen find Christianity hard to comprehend at first? Christianity works like no other philosophy or religion. It's based on a personal relationship with God rather than a set of rules or responsibilities.

The very thing that makes Christianity so confusing to our teenager also makes it appealing. Any attempt to reduce Christianity to something that a kid can understand and embrace without penetrating study and inquiry, in the end reduces Christianity to something that could never command her loyalty for a lifetime.

We must allow teens time to study. Only personal study will give the information they need to envision what a life of faith actually looks like, and what it will cost. Then, and only then, will they be ready for a test drive, the next step in faith development.

Stage 4: *Testing a God the teen doesn't know is trustworthy*

Almost every teenager who actually takes the time to study authentic Christianity eventually will progress to Stage 4.

Paul declared, "I . . . am convinced that he is able to guard what I have entrusted to him for that day" (2 Timothy 1:12). How did Paul become convinced that his commitment to Christ wouldn't be wasted? Why did Paul know that when he trusted God he wouldn't be disappointed? He learned by turning to Christ for help in numerous situations, finding that God really could be trusted.

Teen's question: How much can I trust God?

The question that our teen asks at this stage is, "How much can I really trust Jesus Christ? Can I trust Him with my dating life? Can I trust Him with my friendships? Can I trust Him with my relationship with my parents? How much can I really trust Him?"

Parent's response: Encourage the teen to find out firsthand.

Instead of answering the question for them, it's much more powerful to invite teens to encounter God personally. We might say, "Why don't you experiment and find out for yourself how much you can trust Him?"

We as parents never have to fear what will happen if our teenager chooses to put herself in Christ's hands. Time after time, the psalmists declared with confidence what happens when individuals entrust themselves to God:

> I sought the LORD, and he answered me; he delivered me from all my fears. Those who look to him are radiant; their faces are never covered with shame. This poor man called, and the LORD heard him; he saved him out of all his troubles. The angel of the LORD encamps around those who fear him, and he delivers them. Taste and see that the LORD is good; blessed is the man who takes refuge in him (Psalm 34:4–8).

Encouraging our teen to "test" God to see if she can trust Him does not mean inviting her to jump off tall buildings to see if God will keep her from splattering on the ground. Nor does it mean trusting Christ to cover a check that she writes without sufficient funds in the bank.

The only kind of testing that deepens a teen's faith in God is stepping out to obey a biblical command that terrifies her. Often, a teen's first personal encounter with Jesus Christ occurs when she begins to test God in this way.

As kids study God's Word at Stage 3, they will, no doubt, encounter many of God's commands that scare them because these commands look like they could destroy a kid.

Marti and Mike

Although Marti, a high school sophomore, had grown up around church and studied a lot about God, she had never been serious about Christianity. She never had to trust God with anything scary before. However, recent events were now forcing her to turn to Christ for help.

Her father left her mother before Marti's birth, so Marti never knew him. Her mother was a lonely, depressed woman who abused alcohol to ease her pain.

For most of her childhood Marti was preoccupied with trying to hold things together at home by never being a bother to her mother and by doing her best to make Mom proud. This strategy worked until high school. Then Marti's loneliness overtook her. She longed for a family like those that most of her friends enjoyed. She knew something vital was missing.

In her desperation, Marti decided to take a second look at Christianity. As a high school freshman, she started attending the youth group meetings and soon began avidly studying the Bible on her own. She wanted to believe everything she was hearing. However, she couldn't understand one thing. If God loved her, why wouldn't He help her mother?

At the church youth group, Marti met Mike, who quickly befriended her. Within a few months, the two became close friends. For the first time, Marti felt really loved and wanted by both Mike and God.

She was sure that Mike was a gift from God—until he started to pressure her to have sex with him. That's when Marti was forced to decide whether to put God to the test or not.

Could she really trust Christ with her relationship with Mike? If she took a stand and refused to have sexual relations with him, would she lose him and be all alone again? That sounded like a fate worse than death. If she lost Mike, would another boy ever want her?

Marti faced a terrifying decision. Could she trust Christ to be enough if she had to face the same lonely existence her mother endured?

Finally, Marti decided to trust everything to Christ. She took a stand with Mike. He got mad and told Marti it was all over between them.

That was the day Christ became a real person to Marti. God didn't disappoint her. As she turned to God with her grief, she found the father and friend she'd always wanted.

At this point she also realized that all along Christ had wanted to help her mother. He was just waiting for an invitation. Marti finally knew for herself that Christ was the person He claimed to be. Her faith began to sprout. Marti learned that testing God always involves a scary step of obedience.

Without such a step, Christ remains little more than an impersonal figure from the Bible to our teens. Perhaps they will revere God as somebody great, but they will never embrace Christ as their most precious friend—not until they discover through personal experience that God can be trusted more than any friend.

Stage 5: *Embracing a God whom the teen doesn't want to fail*

Possibly, this was the stage where Timothy was when Paul wrote the letters that bear Timothy's name. By this time, Timothy was a man in his thirties or forties.

It's important that we as parents keep in mind that teens don't have to go through all seven stages by the time they graduate from high school. Faith can continue to grow throughout our child's adult years.

Teen's question: Can I be trusted?

At this stage, our adolescent's attention shifts. Before, she was asking probing questions about God. Now, she starts to examine herself.

As teenagers wrestle with the decision to embrace Christ as Lord and friend, they ask, "Do I really have what it takes to keep a commitment to God? Can I be the kind of person I want to be for Christ?"

Often, a teen holds off embracing Christ—not because she doesn't trust God, but because she doesn't trust herself.

Parent's response: None of us can.

Often, a teenager won't fully commit herself to Christ because she knows she doesn't have what it takes to keep such a commitment. But, what she fails to recognize is that none of us do. That's why, as she is asking this question, we are wise to respond by disclosing our own humanness to our teen. We might say, "You know, so many days I wonder why Christ puts up with me, too. I fail Him so often. Take this afternoon, for example. . . . Although my commitment to Him falters at times, His commitment to me never does. That's why the foundation of our faith must be His commitment to us, not ours to Him."

Randy, the rebel

On a youth-group trip, Randy made one decision after another to disobey the sponsors. That evening, as they returned home, the group stopped at a fast-food restaurant. One of the sponsors took Randy aside and asked him why he had consistently disobeyed nearly every instruction that day.

"I guess you could say I'm a rebel—a rebel without a cause."

The sponsor didn't laugh. Instead, he said, "You're not the only rebel here. During this day, I've gotten angry, been critical of you guys, and gossiped about a fellow leader. I've failed God miserably. Today, I wasn't better than you were—as far as God is concerned. We're both in the same boat when it comes to sinning. Maybe the only difference between us is that I don't like being a rebel, but you seem to enjoy it.

"Oh, I used to enjoy it, like you," the sponsor continued, "until I realized how much my rebellion hurt God—and other people, too. That's when I discovered something that's far more enjoyable than rebellion. Forgiveness! It's great. I've already had the chance to enjoy it a lot today. Christ gives it away for free. You ought to try it. It makes a big difference!"

Randy was stunned. No one had ever talked to him like that. The sponsor had seen right through him. He knew Randy struggled with his commitment to Christ because he felt like such a failure. The sponsor's words that evening helped remove a big obstacle from Randy's relationship with God. Randy discovered that even as a failure, Christ still wanted him.

This may be the greatest truth we can ever communicate to our teenager. As she considers embracing Christ, she needs to know that failing Him will be inevitable. Christ knows that and still wants her. Once a teenager realizes this, she's eager to tell others.

Stage 6: *Spreading the word about a God others don't know*

A kid will begin to spontaneously talk to others about her faith in Christ only after she has come to know and trust Him as an intimate friend. This is why Paul could say, "I am not ashamed, because I know whom I have believed" (2 Timothy 1:12).

Teen's question: How can I get others to want God?

Once a teenager begins to spread her faith to others, new questions occupy her thinking: How can I get Christ to mean as much to others as He does to me? Will Christ make the same difference in their lives as He does in mine?

A teenager soon discovers this is not easy. Seldom is she able to get Christ to mean as much to others as He does to her.

As a teen moves into this stage, she realizes how few people in this world really care anything about Christ—even others who call themselves Christians. It makes her feel alone, and she starts to wonder, *If nobody else believes in Christ, then is He even real? Have I imagined this whole thing? Is there something weird about me?*

When a teenager attempts to spread her faith, her sense of alienation from the rest of the world will only increase, along with the realization of how different she is from most everyone else. But, if she is able to continue against the tide of public opinion, her faith will develop a whole new depth.

Parent's response: Get her talking to God

There are many examples of men and women in the Scriptures who came up against brick walls in spreading their faith.

Elijah, for example, had just experienced a glorious victory against all the prophets of Baal when he found out that Jezebel was on her way to kill him. So, he fled for days into the wilderness where, discouraged and exhausted, he told God how alone he felt. Elijah's discouragement led to an incredible encounter with God.

Many of the richest encounters men and women in the Bible had with God occurred when they brought their frustrations directly to Him.

As today's teens encounter opposition in spreading their faith, wise parents encourage them to voice their frustrations directly to God. Anytime we can get a desperate teenager talking to God—even if she's talking to Him in an angry way—her faith will deepen. God not only inhabits the praise of his people, but he also inhabits their pleas.

The result? As our teen experiences opposition in spreading her faith, she is forced to move to a new stage in her spiritual development—suffering for Christ.

Stage 7: *Suffering for a God who is always with the teen*

At this stage, a teenager chooses to do what Paul invited Timothy to do in 2 Timothy 1:8: "Join with me in suffering for the gospel." Even at the writing of this letter, Paul knew Timothy still needed to grow in his faith. He wasn't yet at Stage 7.

Suffering for Christ is something that God almost always calls individuals to do alone. That's why no one will progress to this stage unless she is convinced in her soul that Christ walks with her and will never leave her.

Teen's question: What if I lose everything?

At this stage, a teen has to ask, "Is Jesus Christ enough if I lose everything else? Will He still love me even though I lose all my possessions, my reputation, my friends? Are His presence, His love, and His power really all I need?"

Parent's response: No glib answers.

At times of suffering and loss, our teenager needs and wants more from us than glib answers. She wants us to show her through our own experiences of suffering how we find comfort and strength from Christ.

For this reason Paul was always transparent with Timothy about his own sufferings. "You . . . know all about my . . . persecutions, sufferings—what kinds of things happened to me in Antioch, Iconium and Lystra, the persecutions I endured" (2 Timothy 3:10–11).

By talking about these trials, Paul was preparing Timothy for the sufferings that Christ would someday call Timothy to endure. "In fact, everyone who wants to live a godly life in Christ Jesus will be persecuted" (2 Timothy 3:12).

Perhaps the most valuable thing Paul ever did for Timothy was to let him observe how Paul himself handled suffering. "At my first defense, no one came to my support, but everyone deserted me. . . . But the Lord stood at my side and gave me strength. . . . And I was delivered from the lion's mouth" (2 Timothy 4:16–17).

From time to time even before adulthood, kids will be confronted with trials and hardships. At these times, like no other, they will draw upon the lessons and examples they witnessed as they watched us go through hard times. To a large degree, they will attempt to weather difficulties in the same way we have.

So, we must ask ourselves, What lesson will my teen learn about Christ by watching me endure suffering? Will she learn that Christ always stands at my side and gives me the strength I need? Or, will she come to believe that Christ isn't enough when she really needs Him—that He can't be trusted after all?

The Stage 7 opportunities to suffer as a Christian, once again will test our teen's faith. If, in the midst of the trials, she clings to Christ, her faith will deepen even more as she discovers that Christ *is* enough. He really is worth suffering for.

At this point, the roots of faith are substantial—too extensive for anyone or anything to pull out. Our teen's faith is *now* a strong structure—one that is ready to last a lifetime.

Five

Faith-Building Skills Our
Teen Must Learn

It is estimated that a teenager must learn at least a thousand different skills to be ready for adult life. Maintaining good health and hygiene requires dozens of skills. Managing money involves over fifty skills. And driving a car entails mastering seventy-two separate skills.

How many skills has our teen already mastered? Hundreds, no doubt. And yet, many more must be imparted to him in the few critical years left before our teen becomes totally independent of us.

As parents, we normally assume responsibility for making sure our child learns the skills needed to be competent and responsible. Many of us naturally do this, even in the area of our teen's faith.

We often emphasize and reinforce in our kids the basic skills stressed in church, such as prayer, Bible study, witnessing, Scripture memory, and tithing.

These skills are important, to be sure. However, they aren't the only skills critical to our teenager's faith development. Often, the skills most needed for our teen to live a life of faith aren't viewed as "spiritual" skills, yet they are foundational to a teen's Christian experience.

Sixty-six and out!

When Jeff was in first grade, there was a contest at church to help kids learn the names of the Old and New Testament books of the Bible. Any kid who could memorize all sixty-six names would get a colorful set of ribbons glued into his Bible.

Jeff worked very hard to memorize all sixty-six names and earn the ribbons. Finally, the day arrived, and Jeff successfully recited them in order to his Sunday school teacher.

But, while gluing the ribbons into Jeff's Bible, the teacher said something that horrified him. "From now on, whenever the pastor sees you carrying your Bible with these ribbons streaming out, he'll ask you to recite the books of the Bible to him."

That was the last time Jeff went to church for over ten years!

In high school, a friend invited Jeff to give his life to Christ. Jeff struggled with this decision for weeks. He knew it was a serious matter. He felt unqualified to be a Christian. After all, he couldn't remember the books of the Bible he'd once memorized, and he wasn't good at praying out loud. These were the kinds of skills he felt he needed in order to be a Christian.

Jeff's friend showed Jeff that he didn't have to qualify to be a Christian. Christ wanted Jeff just the way he was. Knowing that freed Jeff to accept Christ's invitation to follow Him.

Later, when Jeff began to study the Bible as a new Christian, he discovered many things God called him to do, but he was surprised to find out that he was already well equipped to do them. Most of the skills required to serve Christ were not ones learned in church. They were skills Jeff had learned at home from his parents, never dreaming that these skills had anything to do with God or the Christian life.

Picking camp counselors

Jim had the responsibility for a large church camp, and he hired high school and college students from his church to work as counselors and staff. With hundreds of church kids and underprivileged youth from the community attending the camp each summer, it was critical to have a skilled counseling staff.

After supervising the hiring process for several years, Jim developed a profile of the counselor who was most effective in this ministry. The kids who grew up in the church and had the most Bible knowledge weren't necessarily the most effective youth workers.

The skills that made kids effective in ministry were skills that might not ordinarily be thought of as "spiritual skills." Yet, they are spiritual skills—faith-building skills needed any time anyone attempts genuine ministry in the name of Christ.

Paul helped Timothy develop these skills as a young man, and we as parents are responsible to help our teen develop these same foundational skills.

Warning: *These skills can be misapplied.* While helping our teen develop the skills needed for a life of faith, we must be careful not to teach him that his life depends on how well he uses them. Teenagers can easily get the impression that the purpose of these skills is to get something for themselves, rather than to love others.

The guidance counselor's speech

Many parents have borrowed the standard guidance counselor speech that has long haunted juniors and seniors in high school. It goes like this:

"Don't you realize that if you fail to get good grades in high school, you'll never get into a good college? And, if you don't get into a good college, you'll never be able to get a decent job. And, if you can't get a decent job, you won't amount to anything. Your happiness depends on how well you achieve, or how skillful you are!" The last sentence may not actually be spoken, but that's what a teenager hears.

If he hears this speech enough, our kid can come to believe that personal success is the god he must worship and build his life upon.

Skills must be taught for the right purpose

Parents face the challenge of teaching our teen the foundational skills he'll need to love others and serve Christ— without teaching him to use these skills to find his own personal happiness.

For this reason, it's important to sit down with our teen and clearly explain why we're teaching him these things. We might say, "God has given you some wonderful gifts—a fantastic mind and many other abilities. But do you know why He has given these abilities to you? God gave these gifts to you so that someday, if you want to, you can use them to serve Him.

"I know, right now, that might not interest you at all. But, my job as your parent is to help you develop these abilities and skills so that if you want to use them some day to serve God, they'll be there, ready to go. That's why I require you to do well in your responsibilities at school and here at home. You are to develop all your skills and abilities, not to make you or your parents look good, but to love others for Christ."

It's for God's service, not college, career, or marriage, that we as Christian parents must primarily be preparing our kids. Even if our teen isn't a Christian, it's our job to be working with him, helping him to develop his gifts and skills so that if he chooses to serve Christ some day, he will already be prepared.

At the same time, we must teach our teen that God gives us gifts (athletic, academic, musical) for the purpose of ministry, not for the purpose of self-fulfillment. We must not exploit these gifts to get something for ourselves (respect, income, fame). Instead, God calls us to use our abilities to do the work of Christ. This is the call that Paul answered midway through his life. He said, "I thank Christ Jesus our Lord, who has given me strength, that he considered me faithful, appointing me to his service" (1 Timothy 1:12).

It's the same call to service that Paul prepared Timothy to answer and the same call we as Christian parents should prepare our teen to answer.

Developing these skills prepares a teen to answer God's call

A lot of times, a kid chooses not to answer God's call into service simply because he doesn't have the basic skills needed to live a life of faith. An unskilled teen doesn't enjoy serving God if he's not very good at it, so he gives up quickly. He hasn't been equipped for a life of faith.

In 2 Timothy Paul described six foundational skills that equipped Timothy to serve Christ. Imparting these six skills to our teen should be a top priority for us as Christian parents.

Skill #1: *Suffering for something bigger than himself*

The first skill that Paul urges Timothy to use is a skill that good soldiers model. Paul writes, "Endure hardship with us like a good soldier of Christ Jesus. No one serving as a soldier gets involved in civilian affairs—he wants to please his commanding officer" (2 Timothy 2:3–4).

Soldiers learn from the very first day of their basic training to endure hardship in a new way—for the sake of their commander, their fellow soldiers, and their country.

Every teen learns how to suffer hardship for his own sake in order to get what he wants. However, soldiers learn how to suffer for something or someone larger than they. Some might call this the skill of self-sacrifice—learning to sacrifice one's self for another.

Until teenagers learn this skill they don't have the most fundamental skill necessary to love others. How can they begin to love someone until they are capable of enduring hardship or inconvenience for that person?

Although this is a skill every teen should learn before reaching adulthood, many in our culture do not. This is why so few are equipped to be good marriage partners or parents. Although today's teens know a lot about enduring hardship, they know little about doing it for the sake of others.

A high school athlete trains strenuously year round for his sport. He thinks nothing of going out on a Friday night or Saturday afternoon and crashing some other guy as hard as he can, only to get back up and do it again. Even though he finishes the game with broken bones, bruises, and sprains, he can't wait until the next game.

Why does he endure hardship? For selfish reasons. He wants that varsity letter. He wants the prestige that goes with being on the football team. He wants to date the girls who only date football players. Or, he wants the scholarship that will give him a shot at greater fame and fortune.

A young woman starves herself because she wants that slimmer body, believing that her life depends on it. Talk about hardship! She lives with hunger pains day in and day out, not eating—even though food is all around her. It's one thing to starve when there isn't any food available. But, think about the strength it takes to actually starve yourself when all the kids around you are eating constantly.

These teens know how to endure hardship, but it's for nobody but themselves. How different is the suffering that most high school kids endure from the suffering Beth chose while growing up.

Beth's story

When I was growing up I had a very abusive father. He would come home drunk and just rage. Since I was the oldest of five kids, I would always be the one to rescue the others. Sometimes I would literally have to throw my body in front of my dad to keep him from beating them.

For many years, I looked back at all I endured and considered it such a waste. However, recently I've been working with juvenile delinquents. I've started to discover that the suffering I learned to endure for my kid brothers and sisters has ideally equipped me to help the teenagers I now work with.

Many of the adult staff come and go. They last an average of three months. But I've been there about four years. It's really tough working with these kids. I realize the reason I've been able to hang in there has a lot to do with what I learned growing up in an abusive environment.

I learned how to endure hardship for the sake of others. I've found myself even being thankful for the way God used it to teach me to love!

All the time God was developing this skill in Beth, she didn't even know the Lord yet!

Of course, experiencing an abusive home like Beth's isn't the only way a teenager can learn bold love. This skill can be taught through a wide variety of "soldiering" experiences. That's why Paul used the soldier image. "Soldiering" experiences don't require enrolling our teen in military school either. Any time an authority requires a teenager to put someone else's welfare in front of the teen's own, that's a soldiering experience; the teen must subordinate his own interests to someone else's. What a shame it would be if our teen had to enlist in the military to experience this.

How can we as parents provide "soldering" experiences that will equip our kid with this skill? The Bible teaches that human nature never wants to subordinate it's own interests to someone else's (Philippians 2:21). A person only learns this skill by being required to do it. And, of course, that takes authority, the one thing teenagers hate the most.

Parents must endure hardship when they teach this skill

As parents of teenagers, we learn quickly that if we want to be popular with our kids, we cannot use our authority very often. Our teen knows how to make us pay. He argues, pouts, and makes everyone in our home miserable. He has a thousand ways to make it too costly for us to use our authority very often.

If we allow our teen to convince us not to use our authority, he'll never learn to put another person's well-being before his own. He'll never develop the ability to suffer for someone or something larger than himself.

In fact, without authority a teen assumes he is the biggest thing in the world and everything should always revolve around him.

Developing homes that attack self-centeredness

One of the best ways we can teach our teenager this skill is *by requiring him to make sacrifices for his own family members.*

It used to be a practice to keep the sick or elderly members of our families living at home, instead of putting them in nursing homes. What a learning experience in selflessness it was for a child to be called upon to help take care of his own grandmother or grandfather. Can you imagine today's teens giving up their bedrooms for this cause?

Today, in many families children seldom are required to care for anybody but themselves. More and more, homes have become child centered. Mom and Dad constantly subordinate all their interests to their children's interests. All schedules revolve around the kid's soccer practices, dance lessons, and social activities. Parents don't think twice about sacrificing friends, health, even their own spiritual life, to transport and support their kids in all their endeavors.

Is this really loving our teen? When we center our existence around him, when we labor so hard to show him how "special" he is, what is he really learning? He may begin to think, *Because I'm a special person, I really should be served by my world. If Mom and Dad's world revolves around my needs, that's the way the rest of my world should work, too.* This lesson could cripple him for life.

Years later he may come to realize that a vital "muscle" never got exercised the way it should have when he was young. He may discover this weakness in the first years of his marriage when he is asked to do things for which he has no practice, experience, or training.

He never learned the skill of suffering for someone or something larger than himself. Even as an adult, when required to learn this skill or risk losing important relationships, he will still resent it. It won't seem fair.

One of the main reasons missionaries drop out of the ministry is interpersonal conflicts due to selfishness. When they arrive on the field, they have all the Bible knowledge they need. They know how to share the gospel. They can even translate the scriptures from the original languages. The one skill they lack, however, is the skill of putting others ahead of themselves.

This is perhaps one area in which Bible colleges and seminaries are least effective. Teaching someone to endure hardship usually requires more authority than schools or churches have.

Only parents have the authority to require a teenager to endure hardship for the good of others.

Skill #2: *Staying within the boundaries—no matter what*

Paul taught Timothy to stay within the boundaries just as a competitive athlete does. Paul wrote, "If anyone competes as an athlete, he does not receive the victor's crown unless he competes according to the rules" (2 Timothy 2:5).

The dating question

Often, even before our children become teenagers, they begin asking when they can start dating.

How do we know when our teen is ready to handle the responsibilities of dating? The degree to which he has learned to stay within boundaries, no matter what, is a much better criterion for determining dating readiness than chronological age alone.

Teens who begin dating without yet having learned this will be unprepared to handle the pressures dating places on them.

The greatest social pressures (both internal and external) that our teenager will ever experience will come in dating situations. The skill of staying within God's and his parents' boundaries enables him to control his impulses under pressure.

The strongest impulses a kid will ever experience are his sexual impulses. Parents have little opportunity to know if our teen has learned to control his sexual impulses before he starts to date. So, we have to help him develop this skill by teaching him how to control other impulses, such as laziness or anger.

When our kid says, "I'm sixteen now, and you said that when I was sixteen I could start dating," a good response might be, "Now that you're sixteen, dating, just like driving, will be permitted once you demonstrate proficiency at certain skills. Dating requires you to have incredible self-control. When you're able to control the urge to leave your clothes laying wherever you take them off, you'll be showing us that you've developed the kind of self-control you'll need when you start to date."

Athletes on the playing field must always have their impulses under control or risk disqualification and defeat. Despite constant pressure to cheat or find short cuts, they stay within the boundaries, living by the rules of the game in order to win a prize. They could never win that prize by giving in to their natural impulses.

Today, kids could get the wrong impression watching the unsportsmanlike conduct rampant among professional athletes. Some highly paid athletes have disavowed any responsibility as role models for our kids. Paul used the metaphor of an athlete to illustrate this skill for Timothy because, in his day, athletes were great models of self-control.

In order to serve God effectively, we all must control the impulse to go outside God's moral boundaries. Some men and women who have developed great singing, thinking, and speaking skills end up losing the greatest prize of all—the privilege of being used by God in other people's lives—because these men and women never learned to control their impulses.

As parents, we must do all we can to equip our teen with this skill.

Actual athletic experiences can be a good place to start. Athletic competition provides pressure situations in which teens can learn the consequences of not controlling their impulses. Yet, the consequences aren't usually life threatening. When our teen loses his temper or breaks the rules on an athletic field, he quickly learns that if he doesn't play by the rules, he is of no use to anyone.

This is not to say that every teenager should be rostered in a sport. But every teen needs to be coached through experiences in which he pursues a goal under pressure with established boundaries which he cannot violate without immediate, painful consequences.

When a kid is striving to attain something he wants badly, we can teach him the skill of staying within the boundaries no matter what. Even when he fails to reach a particular goal or win a particular game, he can learn that staying within the boundaries wins a more important prize—respect and influence in other people's lives.

Skill #3: *Working hard now for results later*

Paul also directed Timothy's attention to the world of farming to learn this skill. He writes, "The hardworking farmer should be the first to receive a share of the crops" (2 Timothy 2:6).

Farming teaches cause and effect

Farming is the best context for illustrating the principle that rewards usually come over a long period of time through responsible labor. This lesson is more difficult than ever for our teens to learn since most of them grow up a long way from the farm.

Even as infants and toddlers, kids are already asking, "What do I have to do to get what I want?" The kind of parenting they receive as they grow up determines, to a large degree, how they learn to answer this question and what life skills they acquire.

Rarely does a kid naturally come to the conclusion that he has to wait or work hard to get what he wants. Conversely, he often discovers that he can achieve most things without being responsible or waiting. As a result, he never develops the skill of working hard now for rewards later.

Too often, a kid believes it is unfair for anyone to even suggest this idea. He says, in effect, "I ought to have a harvest without having to plant any seeds, without having to do any work, without having to do any watering."

Some have called this a sense of **entitlement:** "I am entitled to get what I want without hard work or waiting."

It is critical during adolescence for teens to connect rewards to responsibility. Unless they make this connection, they will be unable to function effectively in adult roles, and they will be ineffective in serving God. God calls us to work hard for Him—often without immediate rewards. In fact, often we will not experience the rewards for serving God until we get to heaven!

When a kid has no grasp of the reap-what-you-sow principle, then he can't even enjoy God's grace shown to him. To a kid, grace seems like what he's got coming. He may think, *Of course Christ should have died on the cross for me. He created me, He loves me, He owed it to me.*

Today, many of our kids don't know how to enjoy gifts because they believe they deserve everything they get—and more! They've never learned that they only deserve to reap what they've sown.

In farming experiences kids come to realize two truths:

1.   Normally, we reap rewards only when through hard work we have sown something.
2.   We can only reap what we haven't sown when someone shows us grace.

Today, our kids reap the fruits of what *we've sown* through hard work. Usually, they weren't even around to see the sowing.

Many of our teens mistakenly assume that we have what we do because someone gave it to us. They weren't around when we were eating beans and macaroni and cheese every night of the week. They weren't around to see our first apartment with no furniture. They didn't see our early years of sweat and the sacrifice that made possible what we have today.

Years ago, more dads and moms were farmers, and they worked all day long out in the fields where their kids watched their labor and helped. Years ago, more craftsmen worked in their own shops with their kids working at their sides as apprentices. Kids watched their parents labor all day long.

Today, when parents come home tired from work, the kids don't have the foggiest idea why. Rarely does our teenager have the opportunity to observe us sowing. He just sees us reaping. He figures, if we're reaping without sowing, he ought to be able to do that, too.

The job of parents is to design farming experiences that give our teenager the opportunity to experience both feasts and famines directly resulting from his own sowing activities or lack of them.

Sowing activities require our teen to invest effort without immediate gratification. Although teens often resist adults' attempts to engage them in activities that require them to work hard now for rewards later, many report their highest levels of joy, self-esteem, and enthusiasm after participating in such activities. It's good medicine for our teen even though he resists taking it.

In contrast, *reaping activities* give our teen immediate pleasure. Not surprisingly, most kids greatly prefer reaping activities to sowing activities.

Two or three decades ago, teenagers spent approximately 70 percent of their time in *sowing* activities: preparing for the future, building skills, actually doing things which were instrumental to success later in life. They only spent 30 percent of their time in *reaping* activities—things that brought immediate satisfaction or pleasure.

Today, the percentages have flip-flopped. Teenagers spend less than 30 percent of their time in sowing activities and 70 percent or more of their time in reaping activities. Many activities for teens today are designed to give them immediate payoffs, denying them an opportunity to learn the skill of working hard for future rewards.

For example, when a teen is permitted to immediately spend every cent he earns without saving for the future, he never develops the ability to deny himself immediate pleasure for the sake of greater pleasures later.

We can give our kids too much

Parents who are affluent have even a greater challenge in building this skill into their teenager. They have to make a conscious choice, for their kid's sake, to live beneath the standard of living they could afford.

Most of us tend to live at our maximum possible standard of living. We don't deny ourselves things that we can afford (and in many cases even the things we *can't* afford). However, without some hardship, a kid never exercises the character muscles he'll need to serve Christ. Hardship or famine motivates a kid to spend more time in sowing activities than in reaping activities.

Music can be a farming experience

One area that provides abundant opportunities for teaching our teen this skill is music. Developing a musical talent is like farming because it takes lots of hard work before rewards can be reaped. Yet, music practice is one of the greatest sources of conflict between parents and kids.

When we're not committed to helping our kid learn sowing skills, no matter what, we get worn down and stop requiring him to participate in sowing activities. It's imperative that we keep reminding ourselves that there is much more at stake than just learning to play the piano. We're preparing our teen for a life of serving God.

Skill #4: *Doing right when everybody says it's wrong*

Paul encouraged Timothy to be willing to be viewed as a "criminal." He wrote, "Remember Jesus Christ, raised from the dead, descended from David. This is my gospel, for which I am suffering even to the point of being chained like a criminal" (2 Timothy 2:8).

Serving Christ often requires the skill of doing right even when everybody says it's wrong. Christ often calls us to do and say things that others don't understand or agree with.

Joseph had this skill. Look what happened to Joseph in the Old Testament when he dared to speak out. His brothers first tried to shame him into silence. When that didn't work, they treated him like a common criminal, putting him into chains. Still, Joseph kept doing right when others told him it was wrong.

Both Joseph and Paul possessed the skill of suffering for doing right. They developed this skill by taking leadership, stepping out from the crowd, and advocating positions that others criticized.

We can help our teen develop this same skill in formal leadership positions to which they are appointed or elected (student government, church committees, community organizations), or in informal situations (taking a stand during classroom debates, conversations with friends), or questionable practices at work.

Any time a teen declares what he thinks is right in opposition to what others think, he is exercising leadership. As a result, he will eventually experience criticism, ridicule, persecution, and scorn. But, the more he does it, the more skilled he will become.

One of the best ways to help our teenager develop this skill is by encouraging him to jump in and do something about the problems or needs he observes at school, in the community, or in other people's lives. This may mean helping the needy, opposing an unfair practice, or speaking out on a moral issue.

Challenging Fisher

One day Nancy, a high school junior, told her mother, "I'm really concerned about my boyfriend, Fisher. He's having a lot of struggles. He seems confused. He's not getting along with his parents."

"What kind of help do you think he needs?"

"I don't think he has a very close relationship with the Lord," Nancy replied. "I think he needs to realize that a lot of his struggles have to do with that."

"Have you ever talked to him about it?" her mom asked.

"No, I'm afraid of how he'd react."

Nancy's mom advised her daughter to risk it even though Nancy was afraid he might stop dating her. The mother wisely encouraged Nancy to use the same skill Paul urged Timothy to use, regardless of how others might react.

Skill #5: *Putting into his own words what he believes*

Paul recognized that God calls every Christian to be a teacher of others. This requires each of us to learn to put what we believe into words—words that have been carefully crafted to give an accurate picture of God to the world. In urging Timothy to use this skill, Paul wrote, "Do your best to present yourself to God as one approved, a workman who does not need to be ashamed and who correctly handles the word of truth. Avoid godless chatter, because those who indulge in it will become more and more ungodly" (2 Timothy 2:15–16).

Putting what he believes into his own words is a skill that equips our teen for many roles in life. Not only does it enable him to tell others about Christ, but it also enables him to cultivate honest and intimate relationships with others. Without this skill his relationships will remain shallow and deceptive.

Paul also called this skill "speaking the truth in love," and he said that both spiritual growth and healthy relationships in the church depend on it (Ephesians 4:15–16).

This is a weak area for teens

Teenagers generally aren't very good at putting into words what's in their hearts. They need practice and help in learning how to do this. Paul urged Timothy to be a "skilled craftsman" with the words he used to communicate what was in his heart. The best context for crafting convictions into words is teaching opportunities. By encouraging our teen to take a teaching role in which he has to teach what he knows or believes to others, we can help him develop these important communication skills.

Saundra teaches about sex

During the summer before her senior year in high school, Saundra was a camp counselor for a group of junior high girls. This was her first teaching role, her first opportunity for putting into words what she believed. How did it impact her? She writes, "This week, I've been required at least twenty times to put into words what I believe are the biblical standards for sex in dating. Before this week, I don't think I'd ever had to do that. But, every time I tried to explain to one of my girls what I believed the Bible taught about dating, I got better at it."

How a teenager can deepen his own convictions

Every time teenagers have the opportunity to put their beliefs into their own words, their convictions grow stronger and clearer. A kid usually does not internalize what he hears and make it his own until he puts it into his own words and explains it to others.

Often, a kid gets practice at using this skill during debates at school on topics like abortion, evolution, or homosexuality. Wise parents encourage their teen to put his convictions into words as often as possible.

At home, around the meal table, we can encourage our teen to share his opinions and views on various topics, even debate them with us. Even when there are disagreements between a parent and a teen, the parent can still affirm the teen's ability to think and talk about his beliefs. The more we can encourage our teen to talk with us, the more opportunity we have to shape his internal convictions.

A teen who gets practice at home putting his beliefs into words is much more apt to use this skill around his friends. And of course, this not only gives him experience at speaking out what he believes, but it also trains him to speak it out clearly and persuasively.

Churches can help teens develop this skill, too, by inviting them to help teach Sunday school classes or lead Bible studies. Kids who get involved in teaching the Bible to others are much more likely to answer God's call into Christian service when they become adults.

Skill #6: *Choosing what kind of person he wants to be on the inside*

In describing this skill to Timothy, Paul contrasted two kinds of kitchen vessels. "In a large house there are articles not only of gold and silver, but also of wood and clay; some are for noble purposes and some ignoble. If a man cleanses himself from the latter, he will be an instrument for noble purposes, made holy, useful to the Master and prepared to do any good work" (2 Timothy 2:20–21).

Paul knew that God had given his son in the faith, Timothy, an incredible choice (just as He has given it to all of our children). Timothy could choose what kind of vessel he wanted to be—one used for God's noble purposes or a vessel used for his own not-so-noble purposes.

Which is more important?

Most kids know that they have the power to choose who they are outwardly. But, very few know they also have the power to choose who they are inwardly. They believe that the quality of their lives depends much more on the quality of their outer persons, than their inner persons. They have no idea that the opposite is true!

Gary's skin disease

In high school Gary thought that God would never be able to use him much because of who he was outwardly. Gary had an embarrassing disease. Large cysts grew on his face, neck, and back. It was not a typical case of acne. These cysts would swell, erupt, and leave scars.

Often, Gary would be at school when a cyst would rupture and bleed down the side of his face. He went through numerous dermatological treatments, but nothing seemed to help. He figured that since he didn't look like much outwardly, God couldn't use him for much. However, God sent somebody into Gary's life to teach him how little his outward person really mattered.

Gary's family moved just as he was entering his junior year of high school. On the first day at his new school, Gary was shocked to encounter somebody with the same skin disease he had—except this boy had it twenty times worse. To Gary's great surprise, this kid, Hank, was one of the most sought after kids in the high school.

One day after gym class, Hank asked Gary to bandage the cysts that he couldn't reach on his back. Gary took that as an opportunity to ask Hank a question he'd been dying to ask, "Hank, why doesn't it bother you that you have all these cysts? I mean, I have the same problem and I feel like the Phantom of the Opera.

"Gary, my friend," Hank replied. "What I've learned is that if God has his choice between a dirty piece of crystal and a clean peanut butter jar, He'll use the clean peanut butter jar every time.

"I've learned that if I keep clean on the inside, it doesn't matter how I look on the outside. I could look like a peanut butter jar, and God would still use me."

Hank echoed Paul's message to Timothy. Even though Gary had little or no control over his outward appearance, he did have a choice about what kind of person he was on the inside.

Because teenagers are far more concerned about who they are outwardly, they need our help to choose what kind of persons they are on the inside. Without the deliberate use of this skill, our teen will ignore his inner person and never be useful for God's purposes.

The best context for building this skill is decision making. When kids face decisions like whether to go out for a sport, what to do during the summer, or where to go to college, we have the ideal opportunity to call their attention to what kind of person they want to be on the inside. It's not what they decide when they make these decisions. It's why they decide it! The goals that guide a teen's decisions shape the kind of person he is on the inside.

Janet just wants to have fun

Janet was in a quandary, so she went to her youth director. "I've got a big decision I'm wrestling with," she said. "I have to choose between going on a spring trip with the cheerleaders from school or going on the trip with the church. I already asked the cheerleading advisor to tell me all about the school trip. Now I want you to tell me about the church trip. Then I'll decide which one sounds like the most fun."

Seeing a greater issue at stake than what to do for spring break, the youth leader answered with a question of his own, "Janet, do you want to be the type of person who makes big decisions like this just on the basis of fun?"

"What do you mean? What other basis would I use?"

"How about basing your decision on where you can be of

the most service to others? *How* you decide, Janet, is more important than *what* you decide. How you decide will determine what kind of person you are—a person who centers her life strictly around herself or a person who cares more about others than herself. Before you make a big decision like this, it is wise to think first about the kind of person you want to be."

Why is Carl going to college?

Carl was a talented artist, so his pastor was surprised when Carl announced that he had decided to go to Bible college.

"You've been talking for years about going to art school," the pastor replied.

"I know, but I've changed my mind."

"What changed your mind?"

"I've decided to attend Bible college because otherwise the people at church will think that something is wrong with me—that I'm gay or something."

"I don't think whether you go to Bible college or art school is really the most important question," the pastor challenged. "The most important question is, What kind of person do you want to be—the kind of person who makes decisions based on what other people might think or the kind of person who makes decisions based on where you think God can use you the most? What if, from now on, you made every decision based on what other people might think of you? Where would that lead?"

Neither Janet nor Carl had ever been challenged to make a decision based on what kind of person they wanted to be on the inside. Teenagers seldom are.

Another good time to instill this skill in a teen is when someone hurts him. Every teen tends to operate as a nonreflective reactor. If someone hurts him, he decides to hurt that person back. In this way, he becomes a mirror image of others—letting the people around him control what kind of person he is.

As parents, we want to train our teen to stop before he reacts and say, "Wait a minute. How do I choose to respond to this person? If I mirror back to him what he's done to me, then I'm letting him choose what kind of person I'm going to be—the same kind of person he is. I want to be different. I'm going to choose for myself how to respond."

Most of the time, if someone helps a kid take the time to reflect, he chooses to be a very different kind of person than he would on impulse.

These skills prepare a young person to someday answer God's call to service. Without them a young person is less likely to answer the call. Developing these skills is a vital step in guiding our teen to a faith that lasts.

Six

Exposing Our Teen to the Contagious Lives of Passionate Christians

Remember when your children were little? If one got the measles or chicken pox, you probably made sure the other kids spent lots of time with her so they would all be infected at once.

Paul passed on his faith to Timothy in the same manner, recognizing that God's Spirit often uses "carriers" to transmit faith in Jesus Christ from one person to another (2 Timothy 2:1–2). The Christian faith is infectious, and healthy Christians, by nature are contagious.

The chapel speaker

A visiting chapel speaker at a Christian school challenged each member of the student body to get under the discipleship of an older, more mature Christian.

"Find someone you respect because you can see Jesus Christ living in his or her life—perhaps a faculty member," he said. "Spend as much time as you can with that person. Ask that person to teach you everything he or she knows about the Lord."

Little did the school staff realize what this speaker was about to unleash on the faculty of about thirty. After that challenge, ninety percent of the student body went to the same three faculty members.

Why those three? What made them so attractive to the students? Certain lives attract teenagers and others don't. Some Christians' faith is contagious to kids while others seem to scare kids away from Christianity.

Teenagers acquire a new "pair of eyeglasses" as they move into adolescence. They begin to see things they couldn't see as children. Their new vision includes the ability to "see through" people. They can read their character much more effectively than they ever could before. And when they see certain qualities in the lives of adults (even parents or church leaders), kids quickly write those people off.

People who aren't contagious to our kid

In 2 Timothy, Paul listed five characteristics of people who will not be successful in advancing their causes—especially among teenagers. The poorest representatives of Christianity, these people are also the least effective in capturing the loyalties and imaginations of teens.

It's important that we recognize these characteristics and do all we can to keep our kids from identifying these people's traits with Christianity.

Adults who never grew up themselves
The first characteristic that Paul lists is self-centeredness. Although teenagers can be very tolerant of other kids who are self-centered, they are quickly turned off by immature, selfish adults.

Paul wrote that in the last days "people will be lovers of themselves, lovers of money, boastful, proud, . . . ungrateful, . . . [and] conceited" (2 Timothy 3:1–4).

But Paul was also confident that those trying to spread the disease of selfishness would not be accepted. He told Timothy, "They will not get very far because, . . . their folly will be clear to everyone" (2 Timothy 3:9).

According to Paul, people who like to hang out around Christians (especially young or weak ones), sowing seeds of selfishness, have difficulty gathering much of a following because their lives are repulsive. Although they might be able to fool a few folks for a while, people, especially teens, will eventually see through them and reject the toxic lifestyle they spread.

The football star

A church looking for a youth pastor decided it wanted a person skilled in building relationships with kids and getting involved in their lives. They didn't want someone who would just come in with a big program and draw crowds of kids but be unable to cultivate real spiritual maturity in their lives.

Shortly after the search started, an influential member of the board insisted that his son was the perfect candidate for the position. Waving all the interviews and abandoning the criteria they had established, the board decided to put the guy up in front of the kids and see what he could do. They invited him to teach the high school class one Sunday and let the kids vote on him.

He came and taught the sixty-member class. Although he related a number of humorous events from his life, he never once opened the Bible. He told many stories about himself—one football story after another of how God had done "wonderful things through him" as a high school and college player.

The kids enthusiastically voted to have him as their youth pastor. Without further discussion the board offered him the position.

Within a year, the high school group shrank from sixty to five. Understandably concerned, parents and board members began to quiz the kids. The teens agreed in their assessment. "All this guy does is talk about himself. He doesn't care about us. He doesn't ever teach us the Bible. He acts stuck up, like he's still this big football star or something. Even though he's funny and tells great stories, he never asks about us."

Many of the kids dropped out of the group to hold their own Bible study at someone's home.

The kids were fooled by the new youth pastor at first, but he couldn't get away with it very long. They quickly figured out that he was still performing, like he did in high school, to get people to like him. It disgusted the kids.

A television star, rock artist, comedian, or even a youth pastor can get a kid to follow him temporarily if his personality is colorful enough. However, kids study their heroes closely. It doesn't take them long to smell selfishness in a person and be repulsed by it!

Sooner or later, Paul says, "their folly will be evident to everyone."

Adults with poor relationships

A second characteristic that robs people of the influence they could have is unhealthy and destructive relationships. Paul writes that some people are "abusive, disobedient to their parents, ungrateful, unholy, without love, unforgiving, slanderous, without self-control" (2 Timothy 3:2–3).

A teenager finds out a lot about people by watching how they relate to others. In fact, kids are drawn to people more by the quality of their relationships than any other single characteristic. Conversely, kids are more repulsed by adults with destructive relationships than by anything else.

Sheila doesn't believe me anymore

Sheila was a seventeen-year-old junior when her parents sent her for counseling. They were concerned because she was dating non-Christian guys, refusing to go to church, and breaking a number of rules at home and at school.

At the first counseling session, the counselor began to inquire about her parents' concerns. "It's probably no surprise to you that your mom and dad are concerned most of all that you are no longer acting like a Christian. They feel that you've lost your faith. Is that true?"

Sheila got right to the point. "Look, I used to really believe in Christianity. But something's happened in the last few years that has made me decide I don't want anything to do with it. My dad is the one who's always using the God talk around our house, cramming Christianity down our throats. But you should hear the way he talks to all of us. One time I even overheard him cussing at my grandma on the telephone. That finished it for me. If having Christ in your life doesn't at least make you nice, then what good is it? My dad is so rude, so uncaring, so disrespectful. He doesn't like anybody!"

A kid studies her parents' relationships. She's attracted to adults who know how to enjoy other people and build ties of kindness and intimacy with them.

Ask teens what is the most important qualification for being a youth worker, and they'll usually say something like this: "The youth worker should love people and enjoy being with them!"

Dennis' family eats out

Dennis took a job as a server at a Mexican restaurant. Shortly afterward, his family went there for dinner, and Dennis was their server. The family was in a crazy, fun mood, and they sat there for hours, laughing and joking. On the way home, Dennis' mom wondered if the family's jovial mood might have embarrassed Dennis in front of the other servers, whom he was just getting to know.

When Dennis arrived home that night, his mom asked if they had embarrassed him by acting goofy.

"Are you kidding, Mom?" he said. "You guys couldn't have been a better testimony to all of those unsaved people. None of the other servers could believe what they were seeing—a family actually getting along and enjoying each other."

Dennis's family was surprised. None of them were thinking about being a good testimony. If they had, they might have acted differently. But laughing and enjoying one another are attractive qualities, especially to teenagers.

Adults who can't control their own impulses

A third way of recognizing noninfectious personalities is by their addictions. They allow everything but love to rule their lives. Paul described them as brutal, treacherous, and rash, people who scorn holiness and loving relationships in favor of wealth and pleasure (2 Timothy 3:2–4).

In the 1960s many teenagers became disillusioned with the materialism of their parents. They didn't want to become addicted to the material things their parents were addicted to. As a result, they abandoned their parents' values. Unfortunately, they didn't know what to replace them with. Eventually, thousands of them turned to Christ in their search for life. They became known as "Jesus People."

What drove them to Christ was the disgust they felt toward their parents' self-indulgence. One thing that drew them to churches and Christian groups was the freedom from material concerns that the gospel offered them. How sad it is that teenagers are now migrating in the opposite direction. Today, our kids are turned off by the self-indulgence they see among *Christians.*

Lindsey meets the pastor

Lindsey was one of a group of teens from her church who went to help after a Los Angeles riot. Since the area had been decimated by fires, there were very few functioning grocery stores. So Lindsey's church sent workers to distribute food at a church near the flash point of the riot.

Lindsey's group arrived at the distribution center about 8:00 A.M. They worked nonstop for several hours, supplying food to the endless line of needy families.

At about 3:00 P.M., a red Jaguar entered the parking lot, and out of it stepped a man dressed in a three-piece suit. He was wearing a ring on every finger and several gold chains around his neck. Lindsey and the other teenagers from her church were shocked to see this man, who seemed so out of place, walk right into the church and ask everyone to stop what they were doing. "I'm the pastor of this church and I want to say thanks to all you volunteers for the long hours you've worked."

With that, the pastor took two donuts and a cup of coffee, got back into his Jaguar, and left.

Up to that point, Lindsey and her friends couldn't understand why there weren't any teenagers in that church. There were lots of adults and children around, but no teenagers.

The answer to their question came, though, as they watched the pastor's grand entrance and not-so-grand exit. That day they observed the materialism and excess among church leaders that has driven many of today's teenagers away from Christianity.

And church leaders aren't the only ones to blame. It's not unusual to hear a kid say, "My parents make a bigger deal out of money and things than they do about God or anything else!"

The pastor's coffee pot

One teen dropped out of church because she got in trouble for using the wrong coffee pot. When the youth group put on a banquet at church for the senior citizens, she mistakenly prepared the coffee in the pastor's gourmet coffee pot.

When the pastor found out, he hit the ceiling. The teenagers had never seen so much passion as the pastor displayed about his coffee pot. His violent reaction repulsed the teen who made the coffee and convinced her that she didn't want to hear any more of what that pastor had to say.

Adults who practice insincere religion

Next, Paul put his finger on perhaps the most repugnant quality of all. Adults with this characteristic will never gain a following among teenagers. Paul writes that they "[have] a form of godliness but [deny] its power. . . . [They] are always learning but never able to acknowledge the truth. . . . These men oppose the truth—men of depraved minds, who, as far as the faith is concerned, are rejected" (2 Timothy 3:5, 7–8).

My mom's a slut!

Lora, a freshman in high school, had become very withdrawn and refused to go to church anymore, so her parents sent her to a counselor. Without much prodding, Lora volunteered what was bothering her. "My mom's a slut and my dad's a wimp! Watching two people who are supposed to be Christians acting the way they do makes me ashamed to be a Christian myself."

Lora said that she had watched her mother, a counselor and a Bible study leader in the church, flirting and having affairs with other men. She had watched her father react in weak ways, not taking a strong stand to help her mother.

Lora didn't see any power in her parents' lives. She was repulsed by everything they stood for.

When the power to live differently than non-Christians is missing in our lives, our teen has good reason to question the validity of Christianity. Religion without moral power or virtue is never attractive to teenagers.

Adults who are getting worse instead of better

The last quality that repels our teen is a deteriorating or decaying character. In 2 Timothy 3:13 Paul warned Timothy about "impostors [who] go from bad to worse, deceiving and being deceived." These individuals start out trying to deceive everybody around them, but in the end they don't even know the truth about themselves.

Hosea compared the people in his day to people who (without realizing it) were slowly aging—aging spiritually, that is. They were losing their spiritual youth and vitality as they drifted away from a relationship they once had with God. Spiritually, they were in a process of decay.

Downhill dad

Jack, a college sophomore, recalls the spiritual decay he has seen in his father.

> When I was younger, Dad used to be real active in church, and he used to read us Bible stories. But Dad doesn't do that anymore. Most of the time he's too tired to even go to church with us. He just sleeps in on Sundays.
>
> There was a time when Dad even wanted to be a minister. But that doesn't interest him anymore. Dad does things now that I used to hear him teach against. I no longer have a dad I can look up to spiritually!

Fighting parents

Helen, a high school senior, wrote the following in a letter to her sister who was away at college.

> Mom and Dad have changed so much. I remember when they used to be so happy. Now, all they do is fight. Instead of praying and reading the Bible together like they used to, they just scream

at each other. Last weekend I saw Dad throw a water glass at Mom after she cussed at him for flirting with a woman at his office.

Our teen watches us to see if we're getting older or younger on the inside. Paul said, "Though outwardly we are wasting away, yet inwardly we are being renewed day by day" (2 Corinthians 4:16).

A kid is drawn to adults who keep displaying a youthful enthusiasm and zeal for Christ—like we had when we first became Christians—no matter how old we get.

Gene's youthful inner man

One of the most effective youth workers I've ever seen was a man in his sixties named Gene. Every year his youthful enthusiasm for knowing and serving Christ increases. Kids love to be around him because he acts so alive.

Although his outer man is showing signs of aging, his inner man is becoming more and more vibrant. And that's contagious to teenagers!

Since one of the most repulsive sights to teenagers is adults who are dying on the inside, we need to be careful that we aren't among the decaying. We become this way when we start to go to sleep spiritually. Every day we seem to grow a little more numb to anybody's interests but our own, a little less able to recognize what's really going on in our own lives, let alone anybody else's.

People whose lives are contagious

Paul was confident that Timothy would resist the kind of people described above.

First, *their lives were too repulsive.* There's no way Timothy (or any other sane young person) would ever get close enough to become infected by them.

Second, *Timothy had been exposed to the opposite kind of people*—people highly contagious with a passion for Christ! Paul wrote to him, "Continue in what you have learned and have become convinced of, *because you know those from whom you learned it,* and how from infancy you have known the holy Scriptures" (2 Timothy 3:15, emphasis added).

Paul is referring to the kind of life Timothy had observed in his mother, grandmother, and spiritual father (Paul himself). These were people whose lives were contagious for Jesus Christ.

They passed the bug to Timothy by teaching and modeling a life of faith in Christ. From them Timothy acquired a love for Christ—something far more contagious than a love for self.

Paul went on to describe the qualities that made his life and Lois's and Eunice's lives so contagious. And we, as parents, should seek to surround our teenager with adults who display these qualities.

Adults who are transparent

We know Paul was referring to people whose lives were transparent because he said Timothy knew all about them.

Paul is implying that he himself hadn't hidden anything from Timothy. A person who is contagious for Jesus Christ doesn't have anything to hide.

The opposite is true of those in a state of spiritual decay. They have a lot to hide. Consequently, they are distant, aloof, and mysterious to teens.

It's not surprising that most often the kid who wanders away from the faith of her childhood (and stays away from it) is the one who didn't enjoy a warm or open relationship with her parents while growing up. Conversely, a kid who experiences warm, open relationships with her parents is the most likely to follow in their footsteps and embrace their values.

Transparency was one of the most effective tools Paul used to transmit his faith to his spiritual son.

Dad's gone; his daughter's drifting

Mitch was a busy, nationally known youth worker. Once, during a time when one of his daughters was drifting, he realized that the distance between the two of them had increased. Mitch assumed, at first, that she had pulled away from him. But the more he reflected, he realized that all this was going on during a time when he was unusually busy, traveling a lot, under a lot of pressure.

Mitch's daughter's spiritual interests began to rekindle as she became close to two youth workers through a Bible study and a discipleship group sponsored by the church. After the Bible studies, which were held at the couple's home each week, she would sit and talk to them for hours about spiritual things.

As Mitch saw the relationship developing between his daughter and the youth workers, he was thankful and jealous at the same time.

One day Mitch decided to tell his daughter how he felt. "I'm really glad about your relationship with Brett and Suzanne, but I'd like to have a relationship like that with you, too."

"Oh, Dad," she replied, "you're too busy to sit and listen to what I'm thinking."

Encouraging a teenager's faith in Christ cannot be rushed or hurried. Mitch couldn't be a contagious Christian to his daughter if she thought he was too busy to listen to her.

Developing transparency in a relationship (helping a teenager know all about you or finding out all about her) cannot happen without spending time together. This was one of Paul's key strategies for infecting people with a love for Christ.

Adults who are puzzling

A second quality that characterizes a contagious Christian is the puzzling contrast he is to most everyone around him. There's a difference in his life that draws people to him out of curiosity.

Paul reminded Timothy that God did not give him a spirit of fear, like all those around him, but a spirit of power, love and a sound mind (2 Timothy 1:7)—a spirit quite different from others who do not know Christ!

In another letter to Christians who were drifting Paul wrote, "I tell you this, and insist on it in the Lord, that you must no longer live as the Gentiles do" (Ephesians 4:17). Paul was concerned for them because their lives were starting to lose their uniqueness. "Surely you heard of him and were taught in him in accordance with the truth that is in Jesus. You were taught, with regard to your former way of life, to put off your old self" (Ephesians 4:20–22).

According to Paul, Christians should be unique.

Teenagers have an extra sense when it comes to spotting differences. They can smell someone who is different a long way off. Those of us who are merely different on the outside seem weird to kids and they avoid us.

However, those of us who are different because we possess a different kind of spirit or heart than those around us, capture a teenager's attention and respect.

Andy finds a mutant

Shortly after he joined a church youth group, Andy realized he needed help. He went to another high school student, Grant, for help. Grant had no answers for Andy, so he recommended Andy talk to an adult. Andy resisted because he had been deceived and abused by adults his whole life.

After several conversations, Grant convinced Andy that his problems were so serious that he had to tell some adult. "Isn't there some adult you could trust?" Grant asked.

Finally Andy agreed to talk to Ron, a Christian man in the church.

When Grant asked him why he trusted Ron, Andy said, "Well, Ron's different. He's not like other adults. He's a mutant." Andy had sensed a different spirit in Ron—a spirit he thought he could trust.

It's the "mutant Christians" that our kid is often most attracted to. She gravitates to Christians whose lives are so different that they stick out like sore thumbs. That's why Paul could write Timothy and say, in essence, As for you, I'm not worried about your following after non-Christians. Their lives aren't very contagious. I'm confident you're going to live a different kind of life because you've been around "mutants," and they've rubbed off on you.

Paul gives three more qualities of contagious Christians in 2 Timothy 1:7–8. "God has not given us a spirit of fear, but of power and of love and of a sound mind. Therefore do not be ashamed of the testimony of our Lord" (NKJV).

According to Paul, power, love, and wisdom enable us to effectively spread our faith in Christ. They are supernatural qualities given by God's Spirit for this purpose. A contagious Christian has power, love, and wisdom that cannot be explained in natural terms.

When we as Christian adults display these qualities that only Christ can give, we demonstrate for our teen the only genuine path for experiencing warmth (love), weight (power), and height (wisdom). Since God designed teenagers to desire warmth, weight, and height, seeing Christians who are enjoying these qualities makes a strong statement about Christianity to them.

Adults with supernatural power

Living with supernatural power is, in a way, like defying gravity. In our hearts there's a gravitational pull on all of us to live like everyone else does—self-motivated and self-absorbed.

It takes supernatural power to defy the gravitational pull of selfishness. We, of course, are talking about spiritual power, not physical power.

None of us has the physical power to defy the law of gravity for very long. Every one of us could defy it for at least a fraction of a second if we were to jump off the ground. But even the highest-jumping athlete succumbs to gravity eventually.

Just as we are all subject to physical gravity, we're also subject to an internal pull to be selfish people. When we try to resist it by our own power, it just gets stronger and stronger.

Contagious Christians find, in their relationship with Christ, the supernatural power to defy the gravitational pull of their own selfishness and live in a unique way.

The church softball team

Keith's first opportunity to observe this supernatural power at work was on a softball field. He was invited, as a non-Christian high school student, to play on a church softball team. Since Keith had been around softball and baseball his whole life, he thought he knew what to expect: tensions rising, tempers flaring, ordinarily mild-mannered men transformed into finger-pointing, name-calling, umpire haters.

But Keith didn't see any of that when he played with the men from the church. There was something different about how they handled bad calls and rude, obnoxious opposing players. Although they all felt a pull to be rude in return, Keith saw none of the Christian men giving into it. For the first time, Keith thought to himself, *There is something about Christianity that's real.*

Just as watching Paul in pressure situations helped Timothy see Christianity in action, playing softball with these men helped Keith see how Christians can handle pressure. Pressure situations give our teen the best opportunity to see supernatural power at work in our lives. And, it's attractive to kids when they see it!

Adults with supernatural love

Supernatural love, a love that doesn't dry up under the heat of abuse or suffering, also commands a teenager's respect. Paul described this quality in 2 Timothy 3:10–11. "You, however, know all about my teaching, my way of life, my purpose, faith, patience, love, . . . and the persecutions I endured."

Timothy saw a love in Paul that wasn't ordinary, the kind of love that every parent needs in order to love our teens in the midst of all the trouble they cause us.

Not long after puberty strikes, parents discover that it takes far more love to love a teenager than it does a toddler. We need the kind of love that only God can supply, and kids are irresistibly drawn to adults who display it.

Spiked punch at church

The kids in a church youth group set out to change the fact that Mike, their youth pastor, had never drunk alcohol. Volunteering to serve the refreshments at one of the youth group socials, they spiked the punch. That night Mike, along with all the teenagers in the youth group, drank alcohol unknowingly. Many of the kids got sick. And, of course, many of the parents became upset.

All the kids expected to see Mike do something horrible, like hang the offenders up by their toes! But Mike handled it differently. He demonstrated incredible patience and care for them.

On many other occasions, Mike endured great hardships working with these kids. He just kept hanging in there with them and kept loving them, opening his home to them despite all the dirty tricks they had played on him. His love bounced back every time.

As the kids watched him, they knew that no human being, in and of himself, could love this way. The quality of Mike's love convinced them there must be something real about Christianity.

Mike's love was contagious. Many of the teens in his youth group ended up giving their lives to Christ because they wanted what Mike had—supernatural love.

Adults with supernatural wisdom

The last quality of a contagious Christian that Paul lists is an "unincumbered mind," a mind that is not weighed down like everyone else's, a mind free to be filled and controlled by a whole new way of thinking—God's way.

Frank and Aaron challenge each other

Frank attended a non-Christian college in the late 1960s. Everybody was shouting revolution—we've got to change the world. Every week Frank would bring a different theory or radical new world-changing philosophy to a Bible study at his older brother, Aaron's, house. And, of course, Frank would run them by Aaron.

Frank could never predict Aaron's reaction, but Aaron was never close-minded or black and white in his thinking. Aaron always listened with a desire to learn more about Frank's ideas. But, Frank always went away less enthralled with the philosophies he was learning and more enticed to know Christ.

Aaron kept guiding Frank toward Christ with simple, yet profound, truths. "You're right, Frank," he would say, "there are a lot of things wrong with the world. But the only way I've found that we can change the world is one life, one heart at a time—introducing them to Christ—because Christ is the only one who can change a person's heart."

Aaron looked at things so differently than Frank's professors and classmates, and even traditional Christians in most churches. Frank saw a man whose thinking was original because it was deeply influenced by his relationship with Christ.

High school and college students value individual and original thinking. Too often, they assume that being a Christian means to stop thinking and follow God as a mindless "ninny." Christians who possess supernatural wisdom shatter this image and offer a kid another strong reason to choose to put their faith in Christ.

As Christian parents, we should ask ourselves how we can surround our teenager with contagious Christians—adults whose faith our teen will want to catch.

Any of us who look at these qualities and think we can produce them on our own are in for a rude awakening. These are characteristics that only Jesus Christ can produce in us as we ask Him to. That's our first step in exposing our kid to a contagious Christian—asking Christ to make us into one.

Passing the "bug" to our kid

The apostle Paul transmitted his faith to Timothy through four infectious practices, just as the Lord Jesus Christ spread the contagion to his disciples. Imitating Christ's example, we can transmit our faith to our kids through practices that mirror, in small ways, God's greatness.

Practice #1—Little incarnations

We use the word little to describe these practices because, as Christ's followers, we do not perform them on the same scale that Christ did. However, as we permit Christ to live through us, our lives more and more resemble the life of Christ on earth through little incarnations, little transfigurations, little crucifixions, and little resurrections.

Paul once declared to the world, "I want to know Christ and the power of his resurrection and the fellowship of sharing in his sufferings, becoming like him in his death" (Philippians 3:10).

For Paul, this began through the little incarnations we are talking about. He wrote,

> Though I am free and belong to no man, I make myself a slave to everyone, to win as many as possible. To the Jews I became like a Jew, to win the Jews. To those under the law I became like one under the law (though I myself am not under the law), so as to win those under the law. To those not having the law I became like one not having the law (though I am not free from God's law but am under Christ's law), so as to win those not having the law. To the weak I became weak, to win the weak. I have become all things to all men so that by all possible means I might save some. I do all this for the sake of the gospel, that I may share in its blessings (1 Corinthians 9:19–23).

How did Jesus Christ reach the world? By taking on the form of those he was trying to reach. He became a man. That's incarnation!

Paul followed Christ's example and became "incarnated" in the lesser ways that were available to him. He always tried to take on the form of those he was trying to reach win for Christ. To reach the weak, he became like the weak. To reach those under the law, he became like those under the law. These were little incarnations.

However, when Paul wanted to reach a person or group for Christ, he couldn't change his ethnicity, age, or physical features. In the same way, there are areas we can't change when we're trying to reach our teenager. But Paul was able to practice little incarnations by entering other people's worlds, adopting some of their practices, and learning to speak their languages. These same avenues are available today to Christian parents and youth workers who want to reach kids.

Entering our teenager's world

It's impossible to reach Muslims for Christ without going to a Muslim country or at least places where Muslims hang out. If we put up a sign, Muslim Revival, on the front of our neighborhood church, how many Muslims would see it and attend? The idea is absurd. We know we have to go to them, to their world.

In many ways, it's just as absurd to expect our teenager to respond to Teen Night signs in our church yards or bulletins.

Tone-deaf youth pastor

Mark's family was desperately trying to get him to come to church, but nothing worked. Mark's whole world revolved around playing his guitar for a rock group. The youth pastor realized no one would ever reach Mark unless someone first entered Mark's world.

Mark teaches guitar, thought the youth pastor. *I'm tone deaf. But I could sure use some guitar lessons from Mark.*

So, he went to the church board and asked the board to pay for some guitar lessons. To his surprise, they readily agreed to the lessons as a way of reaching out to Mark.

After just four lessons, Mark had had enough of the tone-deaf youth pastor. "OK, Pastor, here's the deal. If you will stop coming to me for guitar lessons, I'll come to church." That was the first step in reaching Mark for Christ. It was the only way the youth pastor could think of to enter Mark's world and communicate the love of Christ to him.

Adopting her practices

The teenagers in every community have a culture of their own. In Ocala, Florida, the place to meet and hang out is completely different than in Torrance, California. In Akron, Ohio, the teen fashion look is completely different from that in Newtown, Pennsylvania. Adults aren't generally aware that even within the same community, there are numerous teen sub-cultures.

While it's not possible for Christian parents or adults to adopt all the practices of our teen's culture, it's important that we adopt some.

Wayne's world didn't include basketball

When Wayne was growing up, his older brother, Lee, was a basketball star. Whenever Wayne played with him, Lee would cram the ball down Wayne's throat. Lee and his friends were generally two feet taller than Wayne. As a result, Wayne never developed much interest or ability in basketball because, to Wayne, basketball was synonymous with humiliation.

However, later on, as a Christian social worker, Wayne found himself in a community where all the kids played basketball. In an attempt to adopt this practice, he played with them and soon discovered that no one on the court ever passed him the ball. The reason? Every time Wayne got the ball, he would either dribble it off his foot or throw it out of bounds.

Wayne realized that in order to reach these kids he was going to have to learn something about basketball. That summer he paid a college basketball player to tutor him every morning at the "Y."

At first Wayne couldn't even score a point against his tutor. By fall, however, Wayne was beating him in one-on-one.

That fall, Wayne showed up at the courts in the park to play ball with the kids. At first none of them wanted him on their team, but with a little coaxing, they finally let Wayne play. That afternoon, Wayne practiced incarnation right before their eyes. None of them could get over the fact that Wayne had learned to play basketball just so he could be with them.

Speaking a teen's language

By speaking her language, we don't mean that we pick up our teen's jargon. Rather, we mean that we talk to her about things she has experienced—things she can relate to.

Dad speaks at a sports rally

Because he had three daughters in the high school youth group, Wes was asked to speak at a sports rally the church was sponsoring. What was Wes to do? He decided not to use any of their jargon. He didn't even know what it was. Instead, he talked to them about his faith in Christ through experiences with which they were familiar.

Wes told them about an experience he had in high school, just after he became a Christian. One of the girls in his youth group invited him over to her house to study.

When he arrived, Wes discovered that her parents were not home. She had the lights turned down low and was wearing the tightest cashmere sweater he'd ever seen.

As Wes told them this story at the rally, you could have heard a pin drop. He was speaking their language.

Wes went on to tell them about his discovery that night that there was more power available in Christ than he ever thought possible. God gave him the power to resist that temptation and walk away.

How can we talk to our own teen about Christ in her own language? How can we teach her about Christ in words and experiences that she understands? She isn't struggling with taxes, like we are. She's struggling with other stuff. Showing her how to find Christ's help in her own struggles is one way to experience "little incarnations" for her.

Practice #2—Little transfigurations

In the Bible, we read about a time when Christ was transfigured right in front of His disciples. They saw Him for a moment in His complete splendor, just as all of us will someday see Him in heaven.

Our transfigurations in this life will never be that complete or as sudden. But they can be almost as dramatic for our teen. Paul told Timothy, "Be diligent in [your teachings]; give yourself wholly to them, so that everyone may see your progress. . . . If you do, you will save both yourself and your hearers" (1 Timothy 4:15–16).

Paul taught Timothy that one of the best ways to reach people was to let them see Christ changing (or transfiguring) his life right before their eyes. Nothing can be a more powerful tool for infecting our teen with a love for Christ than letting her watch God change our lives!

The best canoes

Vance discovered how true this is when he took a canoe trip with his junior high school son.

As the fathers and sons stood on the bank the first morning, receiving some canoeing instructions, Vance noticed that all but two of the canoes were dented. He knew that the dented ones would be the hardest to paddle and steer, so he leaned over to his son and whispered: "Look, as soon as the instructor says, 'Get in the canoes,' move with me as fast as you can to number three. It's the best canoe!"

Sure enough, Vance and his son got to canoe number three before anyone else did, and they were able to canoe faster and easier than everyone else all day.

That night, in the hotel room, Vance decided to read the Bible with his son. Quite unplanned, they found themselves reading from Philippians 2:3–4, "Do nothing out of selfish ambition or vain conceit, but in humility consider others better than yourselves. Each of you should look not only to your own interests, but also to the interests of others."

"You know, Dad," said Vance's son, "I was thinking about our picking the best canoe today. Isn't that what the Bible calls looking out for your own interests?"

Vance felt harpooned by his son's words. That night, Vance prayed a lot more than he slept.

The next day, as they stood on the same river bank waiting to get into a canoe, Vance leaned over and said, "Son, let's take one of the dented canoes today and give the other guys a break."

His son smiled. He had just witnessed a little transfiguration in his dad right before his eyes.

Researchers have compared the effects that both *coping models* and *mastery models* have on learning. Mastery models demonstrate, without flaw or error, the skill students are supposed to learn. Coping models demonstrate the skill imperfectly, but with improvement on each attempt.

The study conclusively found that students learn more from coping models. Seeing the skill demonstrated by imperfect but improving models persuaded the students that perhaps they could learn it. However, watching a mastery model tended to intimidate them.

Perhaps this is why God chose to put coping models in every home instead of mastery models. Through little transfigurations, we become coping models for our teenager.

Practice #3—Little crucifixions

These are experiences in which contagious Christians risk their lives or safety in order to serve Christ. Paul described such an experience to his son in the faith. "At my first defense [before Caesar], no one came to my support, but everyone deserted me. . . . But the Lord stood at my side and gave me strength, so that through me the message might be fully proclaimed" (2 Timothy 4:16–17).

Timothy had opportunities to observe Paul experience little crucifixions on many occasions. Nothing persuaded Timothy of Christ's worth more than seeing his spiritual father willingly endure mistreatment for Christ.

Scott watched his abandoned mother

Scott, a university campus evangelist, traces his decision to follow Christ back to something he saw in his mother.

When Scott was in the ninth grade, his father renounced Christianity and abandoned Scott and his mother. Scott's mother was devastated. Heartbroken from being deserted by her husband, she also had to file bankruptcy because of the near poverty condition he left them in.

Scott observed his mother endure it all. Through the whole ordeal, what Scott remembers most was his mother's unshakable commitment not to do what his father did—trade Christianity for whatever would give immediate relief from the pain.

Instead, his mother clung to Christ for the strength, dignity, and integrity to handle all of her husband's harassment.

Scott saw her go to the cross time after time to preserve a Christian home for him. As a teenager, he didn't have to think long about whose footsteps he wanted to follow. He was drawn to the strength he saw in his mother.

As parents, we too often fail to let our teenagers see us endure suffering. We think we should protect our kids from the pain we suffer as Christians, thinking that it might hurt them or turn them off. Seldom is this the case, however. Teenagers are drawn to adults who are willing to suffer for what they believe.

Practice #4—Little resurrections

A little resurrection occurs any time God gives a Christian the power to overcome a physical, emotional, or moral disaster. Paul was telling Timothy about a little resurrection in his life when he wrote, "I was delivered from the lion's mouth. The Lord will rescue me from every evil attack and will bring me safely to his heavenly kingdom" (2 Timothy 4:17–18).

A standing ovation

Phil was a college instructor when he suffered a brain aneurysm, which left over half of his body and face paralyzed. His recovery was slow and incredibly arduous. Despite his extensive physical limitations, Phil continued his active ministry as a husband, father, and college professor.

One day, Phil was invited to speak to the student body at chapel. He could hardly read because the left side of his face was paralyzed, and he had great difficulty in speaking.

But Phil accepted the invitation to speak to what can be the hardest of all audiences—college students. When he was finished, he received a standing ovation, an ovation more for Phil's life than for his words.

To adolescents our life speaks much louder than our words.

Seeing someone suffer through a disaster like Phil did and come out stronger than ever for Jesus Christ captivates kids. God often gives us opportunities, while our teen is still living with us, to experience disasters and little resurrections. It's one of the most effective ways to give a kid a glimpse of the resurrection power of Jesus Christ.

The disasters parents experience come in many different forms. Some of us experience physical disasters (cancer, floods, or unemployment). Others experience emotional disasters (loss of a loved one, betrayal from a friend). And some of us, by committing acts of dishonesty or immorality, experience moral disasters. But God can use even moral disasters to woo the heart of our teenager to Him, especially when she sees us find the power from Christ to honestly acknowledge our failures and recover from them.

Contagious Christians are not perfect Christians! Our faith becomes infectious when our kid sees Christ alive and active in us through little incarnations, transfigurations, crucifixions, and resurrections. These are some of our strongest tools for guiding our teen to a faith that lasts.

Seven

Inoculating Our Teen Against the Enemies of Christ

There's a story line that played itself out in dozens of boom towns in America's "Wild West" days.

The town grows up out of nowhere and booms because of a new industry in the area—a new mine, railroad, government installation, or land rush.

For several years, the town has a crazy, lurching, spurting existence as it shoots up from nothing to a sprawling collection of rough, inexpensive frame buildings. Although the town is still small, new people arrive daily, and activities accelerate at a frenzied pace.

One day an epidemic hits. One by one, people get sick and die. A courageous doctor arrives who starts treating the sick, and inoculating those who aren't.

The doctor systematically works his way through the town (house to house, business to business) offering vaccinations to people who, on the whole, stubbornly refuse to be inoculated against the disease.

Predictably, all but a few families in the town are wiped out. The town never recovers from the disaster. Finally, the mine runs dry or the fort closes or the railroad is redirected, and the town disappears. Today, we find them only on lists of American ghost towns.

Although these towns no longer exist, they provide a backdrop for a great truth: if we don't inoculate ourselves against disease, we risk death; inoculation offers life.

Why inoculation is necessary

Today, we have learned this lesson well, and we make sure our kids get the vaccinations that will make them immune to physical diseases.

Unfortunately, we're not as alert to the need to inoculate our kids against moral disease. This should be just as great a priority because moral diseases are a far greater threat to our teen's health than physical diseases.

The smartest man who ever lived

Solomon was so concerned about teaching moral values to his children that this great Jewish king wrote a moral primer for his own sons three thousand years ago. We can read it in the first nine chapters of Proverbs. Note these sentences:

> Listen, my son, to your father's instruction and do not forsake your mother's teaching. They will be a garland to grace your head and a chain to adorn your neck.
>
> My son, if sinners entice you, do not give in to them. If they say, "Come along with us; let's lie in wait for someone's blood, let's waylay some harmless soul; let's swallow them alive, like the grave, and whole, like those who go down to the pit; we will get all sorts of valuable things and fill our houses with plunder; throw in your lot with us,

and we will share a common purse"—my son, do not go along with them, do not set foot on their paths; for their feet rush into sin, they are swift to shed blood. How useless to spread a net in full view of all the birds! These men lie in wait for their own blood; they waylay only themselves! Such is the end of all who go after ill-gotten gain; it takes away the lives of those who get it (Proverbs 1:8–19).

Solomon's moral primer is full of warnings about the moral diseases people will attempt to give his sons. Solomon's warning inoculated his sons and strengthened their resistance to moral disease.

Inoculation defined

Technically, *inoculation* is the introduction of a disease into a living organism for the purpose of stimulating increased immunity to the disease. Just as there is a way to physically inoculate our teen to preserve his physical health, there is also a way to spiritually inoculate our kid to preserve his moral health.

Inoculation in advertising

Inoculation is a practice that's also used a lot in advertising. Industries long ago discovered that if they told customers in advance who their competitor was and what the competitor would say to try to lure them away, they could strengthen their customers' resistance to rival products and thereby build loyalty.

Paul used inoculation to strengthen Timothy's resistance against the assaults of Christ's enemies. While Timothy was still young in his faith, Paul taught him to recognize and resist error.

It's essential that parents follow Paul's example. There are three reasons why inoculation must be part of our overall strategy for guiding our teen to a faith that lasts.

The nature of Christ's enemies

Christ's enemies are lethal, just like a fatal disease.
Those who want to destroy our kids' faith are infectious, toxic, and potentially lethal. Notice how Paul described them in 2 Timothy 2:17. "Their teaching will spread like gangrene."

We don't hear a lot about gangrene anymore because medical personnel go to great lengths to keep it from occurring. But gangrene can be deadly in a very short time. Once a limb is infected with gangrene, it must be amputated to prevent death.

Who was spreading this gangrene Paul wrote about? Two former Christian leaders. "Hymenaeus and Philetus . . . have wandered away from the truth. They say that the resurrection has already taken place, and they destroy the faith of some" (2 Timothy 2:17–18).

Often, a person within our own church family is in a position to deliver the most lethal blows to our teen's faith— just like Hymenaeus and Philetus were in Paul's day.

Rick's no problem, but Sid?
Shortly after Trent became a Christian his junior year in high school, Satan sent some people into his life to destroy his faith. The one who came closest to destroying Trent's faith was from inside the church.

Trent worked at the YMCA as a lifeguard under the supervision of a college student named Rick. Rick was what the kids at the YMCA called a "party animal." Every weekend he had a different girl on his arm. He had just turned twenty-one and could buy all the alcohol he wanted. His lifestyle seemed attractive to Trent and the other high school staff members.

Rick often chided Trent about his Christian commitment. "Don't you know that you're missing out on life?" he said. "Why don't you let me teach you how to really live!"

Although Rick's jabs hurt, they were never strong enough to shake Trent's faith. Nobody was able to do that until Sid joined the staff at the YMCA.

Sid, a missionary kid, attended a nearby Christian college on what he jokingly referred to as the "seven-year program." He didn't really want to be there, but it was the only school his parents would pay for.

Sid clothed himself as a Christian but was proud of his ability to point out the errors and holes in Christianity. His mission was to get close to new Christians like Trent and turn them away from Christianity.

He avoided belittling or criticizing Trent for his faith. Instead, he approached Trent as a fellow Christian and offered to show him how to be free of all the hang-ups that unnecessarily weigh Christians down—like going to church, believing everything the Bible says, depriving themselves of natural pleasures.

Sid ultimately convinced Trent that most of his Christian beliefs and practices weren't really strengthening his relationship with God. According to Sid, these practices were hurting Trent's "spiritual existence."

Through this approach, Sid accomplished what Rick couldn't do through a frontal attack. Sid's tactic was so effective that Trent didn't even realize he was being lured away from Christ.

Often, the greatest attacks on our teen's faith will come, not from his non-Christian friends, but from the turned-off kids in his own youth group, church, or school. They're the ones who feel the most threatened by a teenager who takes his

Christianity seriously. He reminds them of what they're trying to pretend isn't important. By destroying an on-fire teen's faith, they can avoid thinking about their own relationship with Christ.

Christ's enemies are aggressive

In addition to being lethal, Christ's enemies are relentless in their efforts. They're persistently aggressive. As Paul said, "Their teaching will spread like gangrene." (Gangrene can spread fast!)

In 2 Timothy 3:6 Paul compared Christ's enemies to worms that devour our families while we're not looking. "They are the kind who worm their way into homes and gain control over weak-willed women, who are loaded down with sins."

The subtlety of a back-door attack, however, does not make it less aggressive. The enemies of Christ are relentless as they worm their way into our teenager's life.

Seldom do Christ's enemies come right out and announce, "I'm here to try to talk you out of your faith." Instead, they move into a teen's life disguised as a friend offering something that our teen is craving. This makes them difficult to detect. Paul described them as "evil men and impostors [who] go from bad to worse deceiving and being deceived" (2 Timothy 3:13).

We're going to get Adrienne

Adrienne, an outstanding Christian, took a part-time job at a local company where there were few Christians. Adrienne had no idea that during her first day on the job, several of the boys were betting on who would be the first to befriend her and get her to compromise her faith. It was a deliberate plan.

When we send our Christian sons and daughters out on part-time jobs with an aliveness, innocence, and freshness that can't be found in the world, we must realize that they will become a prime target for the enemies of Christ.

Christ's enemies are versatile

The enemies of our teen have numerous methods of attacking a kid's faith. Here are some that Paul mentioned to Timothy:

- men who teach false doctrines
- some who reject faith and a good conscience
- hypocritical liars, gossips, and busybodies
- some who think godliness is a means of gain
- some who profess knowledge
- those who indulge in godless chatter
- those taken captive to do the devil's will
- lovers of themselves, lovers of pleasure
- those who turn their ears away from the truth
  and turn instead to myths

Some diseases can be transmitted as a result of just a few high-risk behaviors. As a result, even though the disease is deadly, people do not fear it as long as they avoid the two or three dangerous activities. Spiritual infections are not limited to a few methods of transmission. According to Paul, spiritual infections can be transmitted in many ways and by many different carriers.

The enemies of Christ are committed to being versatile—using anything they can to plant thoughts or notions that will destroy faith. The serpent used this approach with Eve, convincing her that God wasn't who He said He was. And Satan has continued to be versatile ever since.

We need to inoculate our kids against Christ's enemies because the enemies are lethal, aggressive, and versatile. But that's only half of the story. Inoculating our kids is also important because of the nature of adolescence.

The nature of adolescence

Adolescence is a time of independence

The years between twelve and twenty are ones of inquiry and decision. A teenager's greatest task, deciding what kind of person he wants to be for the rest of his life, calls for our teen to pull away from us somewhat, to be independent enough to make this decision on his own.

During this period of inquiry and decision, he will be highly susceptible to influences outside the home, so this is an ideal time for the enemy to try to get to him. Having a minimum of supervision and communication with his parents, our teen is highly vulnerable.

Adolescence is a time of disillusionment

As our teen acquires his adult thinking capacities and begins to look into things more deeply, he perceives flaws and problems he never saw before.

He may become disillusioned with everybody and everything. Feeling as if life in general is cheating him, he may say to himself, "The way that I made life work as a child isn't working for me any longer. I feel betrayed because I was taught that if I didn't cheat and tried real hard, life would be great. At our school the kids who don't cheat are the ones with the biggest problems."

When the rules he learned from us seem to betray him, he will naturally become disgruntled and rebellious. At this stage, his defenses against error and deceit are considerably weakened. He could become attracted to philosophies and lifestyles that are anti-authority and anti-God. Without inoculation, our kid becomes a "sitting duck" for the enemy and his "anti-" propaganda.

The first two reasons for inoculating our teen deal with negatives—to combat the attacks of Christ's enemies and to withstand the pressures of adolescence. The third reason for inoculation is a positive one. It prepares him to accurately evaluate the alternatives to Christianity while he is building his faith.

The nature of faith development

Faith building is a process in which our kid slowly becomes convinced in his own heart about what is true and what he believes about Christ.

By nature, faith develops in the context of choice. If our kid is going to personalize his faith, he has to decide, "This is what I want. Of all the things in this world that I could depend on for life, this is what I want to depend on!"

So a teen must be free to investigate, evaluate, and compare. "As I've looked at what other philosophies and ways of life have to offer, I've decided I want to travel *this* direction. I want to travel the narrow road with Christ."

This means he must be exposed to the alternatives to Christianity and have the freedom to make his own decision about their legitimacy.

We cannot protect our teen from all contact with the enemies of Christ, keeping him in a Christian environment, only knowing Christian people, only exposed to subject matter taught from a Christian perspective. Otherwise, when he reaches his early twenties and has already made all his decisions about life, chances are his Christian commitment will never become personal. It will never last.

Without a sense of choice, a kid's faith can't really deepen. He'll never become fiercely persuaded that this is what he believes in the face of all the choices that confront him.

In the absence of choice, a teenager learns only to conform. He adapts his behavior to fit whatever rules are in force at the time. If any faith exists at all, it's a shallow faith that isn't strong enough to survive adversity or disappointment.

Carl and his dad's cancer

Carl was taught his whole life that if he kept a set of Christian rules, God would protect and bless his life. When Carl was in his second year of college, his dad was diagnosed with cancer and soon died. Carl felt betrayed. He and his whole family had done their best to keep the rules. How could God let this happen?

Carl had never before considered living any other way, following any other set of rules, but in his disillusionment with God, Carl decided to look for a new set of rules that required less and offered more. This decision led him to convert to Islam just a year or so after his dad died.

If we want to impart to our teen a faith that can withstand adversity, then before adversity occurs we must expose him in advance to other ways of life. This inoculates him to error and makes it less appealing when life seems to be falling apart.

Test Case—choosing a standard of living

As our teen goes through adolescence, one of the things he has to decide is what his *standard of living* is going to be. So many other decisions (choice of college, choice of major, choice of occupation, choice of spouse) hinge on this pivotal issue. While choosing his standard for living, he finds many conflicting ideologies competing for his allegiance.

Asceticism?

Some religious and even political philosophies teach that the less we have the better off we'll be.

Hedonism?

Hedonistic philosophies teach the opposite. They say the higher your standard of living, the better!

Authentic Christianity?

What does authentic Christianity have to say to our teen as he's making this decision? Which is better—more or less?

This is the kind of test case that we should encourage our teen to explore.

Christ answers this question by telling our teen that life doesn't depend on his standard of living: "Seek first his kingdom and his righteousness, and all these [necessities] will be added unto you" (Matthew 6:33).

The key isn't how much our kid has but who has him! What controls his heart—a desire to love and serve or a desire to prove something about himself by how much or how little he has?

How can we persuade our teen that life doesn't depend on his standard of living? At times, the trials of life make his standard of living seem all-important.

We can tell him, "It doesn't matter how much money you make, what kind of house you live in, or what kind of car you drive. As long as you keep serving and obeying Christ, He'll take care of you."

But this will never become our teenager's own personal conviction until he has a chance to experience or observe this truth for himself. Hearing us articulate it is not enough!

This is where inoculation comes in. Exposing our adolescent to other kids and families, poor and rich, who practice hedonism, asceticism, and authentic Christianity gives our kid a *basis of comparison* and the *context* he needs to see how little a person's standard of living affects personal contentment and worth. We might call this "broadening our teen's horizons."

If we want our kid's faith to deepen, we must allow his horizons to broaden so that he can observe, even at a young age, how empty and false non-Christian pursuits really are.

In providing this exposure, there's always the danger that our kid may choose to follow some non-Christian philosophy. That's scary. And yet, isn't this the freedom God has given to each of us? He has given us the freedom to choose for ourselves what kind of people we want to be.

True choice always provides for the possibility that people may choose wrong.

Besides, if our son wants to experiment with non-Christian approaches to life, it is better that he do it as a teenager, when he's still under our influence and authority. At this time, the destructive consequences of these choices may not be as great. If we force him to wait until he's an adult to experiment, the consequences can be far more destructive and lasting.

As much as possible, we want to help our teen become disillusioned with the best the enemy has to offer—before the enemy even offers it to him. In this way, our teen's resistance will be strengthened against the enemy's assaults.

Often, the teenager who is the most opposed to using alcohol or drugs is the one who has witnessed firsthand the devastating effects of addiction in his own family or his friends' families. The same is true about the effects of immorality or adultery. Exposure to the real-life drama of people living in rebellion to Christ strengthens a kid's conviction that Christ offers a much better approach to life.

The inoculation process

So, how can we inoculate our teen against spiritual infections? We must first understand what inoculation is not.

Inoculation is not sitting our kids in front of a TV

The worst way to inoculate our teenager against Christ's enemies is by permitting his main exposure to non-Christian philosophies and practices to come through the media. The media seldom portrays the true nature and outcome of the lifestyles it depicts. Too often, it depicts immoral and selfish behavior as glamorous and desirable.

Making the media our teenager's main source of information about Christ's enemies would be like making Hitler's propaganda films our main source of information about Nazi Germany. The media only weaken our teen's resistance to godless philosophies.

Inoculation is not instilling a hate for the enemies of Christ

One of the major mistakes we make as parents is adopting an us-vs.-them mentality that encourages our teen to hate non-Christians.

Barry on the Indian reservation

When Barry, a new Christian, went on a short-term missions trip to an Indian reservation in New Mexico, he found the area overrun by homeless people and migrant workers.

They were camping all around the hot springs north of the reservation. By using the hot springs for bathing, washing clothes, and waste disposal, these people were contaminating and spreading disease through the streams that supplied water to the Indian reservation.

There was already a huge movement in the community (even among the Christians) to drive the homeless and migrant people out of the area. As a young and zealous Christian, Barry believed the key to the problem was to love these people and share Christ with them, rather than be mean or cruel.

Within a week or two, however, some of the Christian leaders in the area talked Barry out of his conviction. Soon, he started to hate the homeless and migrant people too, and found himself saying cruel things to them whenever he passed them on the street. He eventually became involved in a systematic campaign to run them out.

Being taught to hate like that was one of the most destructive experiences Barry ever had. After he returned home, he needed months of counseling to regain his perspective. The hate he learned during the summer started to consume Barry. His heart, which once burned to declare Jesus as the answer to the world's problems, had begun to advocate only a political and social solution.

Inoculation is not instilling a fear of the enemies of Christ

Amy goes on an evangelistic blitz

For four years Amy attended a Christian college. Every Saturday, she and her classmates would board a bus and drive to a state university campus fifty miles away.

They would then form groups of two or three, armed with tracts and Bibles, and attempt to witness to the university students.

After a few hours, they would hurry back to the bus and drive back to their own campus in time to catch the Saturday night movie.

After Amy graduated with an elementary education major, she attempted to find a teaching position in a Christian school. When none opened up, she reluctantly accepted a position in a public school.

After her brief encounters with non-Christians, Amy's fear of them only ballooned. With the hit-and-run tactics of the evangelistic blitzes, she never had the opportunity to build relationships with non-Christians and learn to love them as people. Instead, she acquired a mentality that those people "out there" had the power to take away her faith if she got too close.

As a result, Amy found it awkward to work with non-Christians in her new teaching position. She chose not to talk to the other teachers, and she remained very aloof from the students.

Her conditioning led to a type of isolation that, in the end, made it virtually impossible for her to be a witness in the community. She couldn't have friendships with non-Christians or even good working relationships on the job.

Teaching our kids to fear non-Christians is not what we mean by inoculation.

Inoculation is not teaching our teen to envy the enemies of Christ

It's possible to preach against the enemies of Christ in such a way that we make their lifestyles seem glamorous and exciting to our teenager. We can portray the enemy's activity as so mysterious or so horrible that our teen will be dying to check it out.

Some of us treat school dances as so abominable that if our teen happened to be attending one when Christ returned, we think he'd surely be left behind to go through the tribulation! By barring our kid from ever sticking his head into a school dance, we fuel a burning hunger or curiosity in him to do that very thing.

It would be so much more disarming to say to him, "Go check it out for yourself." When a Christian kid does this, he often comes back saying: "I don't know what the big deal is about a school dance. There sure wasn't much life there!"

Many Christian high school students who have the freedom to go to school dances think they're boring. The kids who don't have that freedom think dances are really exciting, and they are dying to sneak into one.

The enemies of Christ know which kind of kid is more vulnerable to their attacks—not the one who has been inoculated to school dances. It's the one who can only imagine what dances are like and is left envying the kids who get to go.

Inoculation that works

Spiritually healthy fathers in the Bible, like Solomon and Paul, were astonishingly candid with their kids about the enemies of Christ. They put their children in positions where they could get glimpses of three key realities about the enemies of Christ: their true character, their true activities, and their true destiny.

When a teen views firsthand the true character, the real activities and the ultimate destiny of those who oppose Christ, he finds little attraction there. All those things that the enemy uses to draw teens away will lose their luster.

Young Asaph

In the Old Testament, a poet named Asaph described how, as a young man, he almost lost his faith. "As for me, my feet had almost slipped; I had nearly lost my foothold. For I envied the arrogant when I saw the prosperity of the wicked" (Psalm 73:2–3).

This is how our teenager often feels when his only knowledge of the enemy is from a distance or through the media. At a distance it is easy for a kid to envy the arrogant, the enemies of Christ.

Look at Asaph's conclusion after seeing only part of the story. "They have no struggles; their bodies are healthy and strong. They are free from the burdens common to man; they are not plagued by human ills. Therefore, pride is their necklace; they clothe themselves with violence" (Psalm 73:4–6).

That's how the enemies of Christ usually try to portray themselves to our teenager.

In reality, however, the lifestyles of many of today's TV and movie stars make us wonder how they have the energy to get up on stage at all. Their lives are like time bombs ticking away. Their stage presence belies no struggles, but behind the scenes, their lives are a mess. Their personal relationships are falling apart. Their bodies are anything but healthy and strong because of the drugs they've injected or ingested and the diseases they've contracted through multiple sex partners.

But we see none of this on stage.

Although Asaph came close to deserting his faith and following the enemies of Christ, in the end, he resisted the pull. Asaph's own words reflect that it was not less exposure but deeper exposure to the enemies of Christ that brought him to his senses. Getting a glimpse of their true character and their true activities, he writes, "From their callous hearts comes iniquity; the evil conceits of their mind know no limits. They scoff, and speak with malice; in their arrogance they threaten oppression. Their mouths lay claim to heaven, and their tongues take possession of the earth. Therefore their people turn to them and drink up waters in abundance" (Psalm 73:7–10).

Asaph got depressed trying to understand why God would permit people like this to apparently be doing so well. How could God let things go better for them than for him—a guy who had tried to obey God and do what was right?

Once God gave him a glimpse of the destiny in store for these people, Asaph became totally repulsed by their lifestyle. "When I tried to understand all this, it was oppressive to me till I entered the sanctuary of God; then I understood their final destiny. Surely you place them on slippery ground; you cast them down to ruin. How suddenly are they destroyed, completely swept away by terrors" (Psalm 73:16–19).

Asaph came close to stumbling because his information was incomplete. This is the same problem our teen faces today. He becomes attracted to the philosophies and lifestyles of the ungodly because he hasn't seen the whole picture.

Inoculation requires giving our kid the fullest picture we can of the true character, activities, and destiny of the enemies of Christ.

Inoculation involves four tasks

How do we do it? We can inoculate teenagers by strengthening their immunity in four areas: their horizon of observation, their powers of evaluation, their capacity to discern character, and their ability to resist attacks.

Task #1: *Expanding our teen's horizons*

This probably wasn't much of a challenge a hundred years ago. Most Americans lived in small communities where almost no one was a stranger. Everyone knew everything about the people in the community.

When someone chose to live an immoral lifestyle, everyone could see how it affected that person's family and livelihood.

Even the kids, in knowing where this person came from, how he lived, and how his life turned out, learned a lot about character. They could clearly see who were fools and who were wise.

Today, we live in such large communities that people—even the people in our churches—remain strangers to one another. We don't know much about each other. We only get small glimpses of each other's lives and rarely know the full story.

So, our teen has limited horizons—limited opportunity—for observing the true character, activities, and destiny of the enemies of Christ unless they happen to be living in our own home. Often, a teen resolves never to experiment with drugs or wander from Christ after observing the disastrous consequences of drug abuse and drifting in the life of an older brother or sister. After getting the whole picture of such a lifestyle, he decides he wants none of it.

But, the best way parents can expand their teenager's horizon of observation is by involving him in the community, enabling him to observe the lives of a full cross section of society, not just the Christian community. Involvement in the larger community can give him a realistic picture of how the enemies of Christ live.

Learning at the relief organization

After several months of volunteering in a community-relief organization, a college freshman commented, "One thing I'm going to do when I get married is work hard at being the best husband I can be. I've seen the consequences of divorce and immorality. I know what kind of pain it causes. I'm going to do everything I can to avoid ever putting my family through it."

By observing a true cross section of society, this college student concluded that immorality is costly, ugly, anything but glamorous. What a different picture Hollywood portrays! This was an inoculating experience.

As Christians, we must resist the temptation to surround ourselves and our teen only with people who seem to have their lives all together. When we do that, we deny our kid an observation post from which he can learn the real truth about life apart from Christ.

Christian families must find creative ways to maintain involvement in the community, ways that allow our teen to see the real outcome of people's moral choices.

Non-Christian friends

Of course, one of the most natural ways to become involved in the community is to befriend a non-Christian family in our neighborhood. This shatters any illusions our teen might possess about non-Christians. It helps him personally observe that what the Bible says is true about them. Non-Christians are lost and needy. They deserve our compassion.

A church that reaches out

Another creative way to expand our teen's horizons is by becoming involved in a church family that is attempting to reach the community around it. Churches with vision offer numerous opportunities for whole families to get involved.

We might reach out through crisis-pregnancy centers, homes for unwed mothers, soup kitchens, hospital and nursing-home services, teen hot lines, community centers, remodeling projects for needy families, after-school clubs, fund-raising projects for charities, tutoring services, disaster relief, or missions in urban settings.

Task #2: *Expanding our teen's powers of evaluation*

Just expanding our teen's horizons will never be enough, however. At the same time, we must help him evaluate what he's seeing. As we help position him to see more, we want him questioning what he's seeing. We want to cultivate a mood in our homes where our teen can question things out loud and evaluate the claims of the enemies of Christ.

Meals are a great opportunity

It's hard to imagine a better setting for evaluation than a family sitting around the table talking about the everyday events of life. Many of the best thinkers of our day developed their powers of evaluation by interacting with their families over dinner, trying to make sense of their world.

A teenager does not develop his powers of evaluation without ample opportunity to dialogue with adults who are already experienced at scrutinizing the world around them.

The news story of the day

One father decided to pick out a news story from the paper each day that he could discuss with his family at dinner as a way to sharpen his teenager's powers of evaluation. Often, he would choose stories about public figures that his teen knew. Together, they discussed moral dilemmas or consequences these personalities were facing.

Movies, television shows, and events happening to people our families know offer the same opportunities for sharpening our teenager's powers of evaluation.

An adolescent naturally evaluates everything he observes. But, without help from parents, a kid may come to incorrect conclusions. Engaging him in nondefensive and nonthreatening discussions about what he sees helps him make accurate, biblical evaluations of his and other people's experiences.

Task #3: *Expanding our teen's discernment*

Discernment is a type of listening—a listening that searches beneath the messages of a person's words to the messages of his heart and character.

A teenager develops the capacity to discern character when he starts to question what he hears and sees. Asaph developed discernment as he began asking serious questions about the enemies of Christ.

Asaph revisited

In Psalm 73 Asaph brought his questions directly to God. In essence he said, "God, I don't understand. Why are these people getting away with evil? Why does it seem like all the godly people are suffering. This doesn't seem fair!"

As he brought his questions to God, Asaph grew in his capacity to discern the truth about others. We are wise when we encourage our teen to do the same. Discernment of character can only be developed and expanded as a teen courageously asks the questions that life provokes.

Church youth ministries need to encourage kids to bring their burning questions to God and the Bible.

The main reason our kid gets bored in church Bible studies is because the time is spent answering questions that our teen isn't asking.

Life provokes big questions in every teen's mind. However, if our teen never brings these questions to God or the Bible, he will never develop discernment.

Parents can provide their kids opportunities to question during family Bible studies, too.

Task #4: *Expanding our teen's resistance*

One way our teenager can get practice resisting the enemies of Christ is to take a stand at school or attempt to communicate to his peers something he believes.

Meeting at the flag pole

Leslie grew in her capacity to resist the enemy when she and a few friends tried to meet at the flag pole for prayer before school, as Christian kids all across the country were doing that morning.

Leslie's principal broke up the meeting, informing the students they couldn't do this on school property.

Leslie and her friends set out to get the principal's ruling reversed, believing that he was denying them one of their basic rights. They took their appeal to the school board and won. As a result, these teenagers grew in their capacity to resist the attacks of the enemy in college.

Whenever kids get into projects or activities in which they are trying to do something good—something for Christ—they will experience opposition. They will have to resist the enemies of Christ. And they will gain vital skills for handling even greater attacks later in life.

We are wise when we guide our teen into endeavors that provide this training while he's still in high school.

As we expand our kids' horizons of observation, their powers of evaluation, their capacity to discern character, and their ability to resist attacks, we are inoculating them against the enemy. This strategy doesn't guarantee that they'll never drift from their faith, but it will strengthen them to resist the attacks of the enemies of Christ.

Eight

Inviting Our Teen on a
Mission for Christ

Every May the senior class at a Chicago-area Christian high school spends a week at a famous dude ranch in the Colorado mountains. One year, after a barbecue and campfire, that year's group of nearly a hundred teens was heading for the cabins.

However, three of the leaders of the class, in a reflective mood, stayed around the campfire.

Chris was the most outstanding athlete of his class—a soccer star and pitcher on the baseball team. Jena was the lead soloist in the choir, star of the school play, and a leader in student government. Arthur was the most outstanding student. He would be giving the valedictorian's address in a few days.

The three began to reminisce about their class's four rich years together. Finally, Arthur asked, "When you think back to all the activities we've been involved in during high school, what was the most meaningful and memorable?"

The nature sounds of a Colorado evening echoed louder as each person mentally reviewed a full four years of highlights.

Chris was the first to respond. "I've got mine, but see if you can guess it."

"Last fall, when we won the conference championship in soccer for the second straight year?"

"No."

"Your no-hitter this spring against West?"

"No."

"We give up."

"OK, it was the trip the soccer team took to minister to high school kids in Romania," Chris said. "We played some soccer, but the main thing was that we were able to work side by side with the Romanian kids. Also, I was able to share my faith in Christ with kids just like me."

"Wow, that's wild!" said Arthur. "I was thinking of the same type of thing."

Arthur was a merit scholar who got a never-ending supply of praise from students and faculty. He had a great sense of humor and was famous for his impersonations at talent nights. During his junior year, he had assured his place in the school's drama history by going bald for three weeks while playing the part of Daddy Warbucks in *Annie*.

With all these experiences to pick from as his most memorable, Arthur chose instead the Spanish club's trip to Mexico during spring break one year. Arthur and the other kids had worked with needy children in Mexico City, and they saw many won to the Lord. "That was my most memorable experience," said Arthur.

Jena laughed. "Guys, you'll never believe this, but I was thinking of the same type of experience."

Jena had numerous highlights to choose from. She had sung a solo with the school choir at Chicago's Orchestra Hall. Voted "most likely to go to Hollywood" by her class, Jena had been featured in school plays all four years. In addition, she was elected student body president as a senior and set state records in softball.

"It was on choir tour . . ." she teased.

"The one to Europe?"

"No, that was like a performance tour," Jena replied.

"The one to Florida?"

"No, that was a fun tour."

"Not the one to West Virginia?"

"Yes, that's the one. We sang some on that trip, but we mainly worked with the people back in the mountains. Several of us worked with local kids to cut out a softball field at their church. We had Bible studies with the kids, and worked on brush cleanup. We put up and painted a whole new building. We weren't working by ourselves. We worked with other teens—kids from the area.

"We also had an opportunity to share our faith with other kids in the community. We saw lives changed," Jena continued. "What we did was go there and say to the Lord and the people in charge, 'Here I am. I'm ready to do whatever is needed.' That was the first time I'd ever given myself to a project where there was nothing to be gained from it but to work for the Lord. Where I was working, none of the other choir members even knew what I was doing. No publicity. No attention. Just doing something for the Lord because He needed me."

All three of the kids picked a missions trip as their most memorable high school experience. Why? What is there about a missions trip that makes it stand out for kids?

The apostle Paul was always inviting young people along on his missions trips for Christ. It was on these trips that his son in the faith, Timothy, had "proved himself" (Philippians 2:22) and acquired the training and maturity to serve Christ for a lifetime.

Field trips like these are one of the best ways to forge in young people a determination to serve Christ. This key strategy is one that we parents should imitate.

Three elements of Paul's "field trips"

Element #1: *Christ-centered purpose*

Paul's field trips with Timothy were not vacations. They were always planned to pursue Christ's interests in other people's lives. They also gave Timothy a taste of what it meant to be a servant.

A servant pursues the interests of others—not his own. Where do young people learn this today? The best training in how to be a servant is in the context of taking a journey which is specifically planned to pursue the interests of Christ.

Decision in L.A.

When a team of high school students, formed to do summer missions work in the Los Angeles area, arrived at orientation, their first questions weren't, "When are we going to hold street meetings?" or "When are we going to start our children's ministries?" Instead, their questions were, "When are we going to Disneyland?" "When are we going to the beach?" "Are the guys and girls on the team allowed to date each other?"

The leaders faced the challenge of teaching the kids they weren't there to pursue their own interests but, perhaps for the first time in their lives, they were there solely to pursue the interests of Jesus Christ.

An amazing transformation took place that summer. Slowly, the kids began to realize their real mission. Soon, they began to taste what it meant to abandon their self interests in order to help other people know and love Christ.

About a month into the trip, a man from one of the area churches came to the leaders. "I understand you haven't taken these kids to Knott's Berry Farm yet. I can't believe you would bring thirty teenagers to California and not take them to Knott's!"

He pulled a wad of money out of his pocket and insisted the leaders use it to take the team to the well-known tourist attraction the next day.

"The kids are having a team meeting in the back room right now," responded the leader. "Come and ask them if they'd rather go to Knott's tomorrow or go ahead as planned with a day of painting the church and resurfacing the parking lot."

After being introduced to the kids, the man said, "I just think it's a tragedy that you kids have come all the way out here and won't see one of our best attractions. Since you'll be leaving the Southern California area soon, I'd like to pay for all of you to go to Knott's Berry Farm tomorrow."

Immediately, one kid asked if it would cause the group to miss the last day of ministry with this church. When the kids understood that it would, they unanimously decided against Knott's Berry Farm. They chose to work instead.

These kids would never have made that choice the first week of the trip. But, after four weeks of pursuing Christ's interests and finding it more rewarding than living for fun, they quickly chose manual labor over an amusement trip.

On missions for Christ, kids experience the Matthew 6:33 principle: "Seek first his kingdom and his righteousness, and all these things will be given to you." Missions trips can help teens learn that a rewarding life is not built on self-seeking. If they concentrate on knowing and serving Christ, Christ fills their lives with good things.

To give our teen this taste of Christ, we must put her in an environment, at least temporarily, in which her time and activities are centered around interests other than her own. It's like getting her off a drug, in this case the narcotic of self-centeredness.

On missions for Christ, our teen can discover there's much more life in serving Christ than in serving self. However, most of our kids go through their entire adolescence without getting a taste of what it's like to serve Christ's interests before their own.

Very few kids who get an authentic taste of serving Christ will walk away from it. Serving Christ gives teenagers a greater sense of aliveness than anything they have ever experienced before.

Element #2: *A dangerous/uncomfortable setting*

A mission for Christ is a field trip that takes teens out of their safe, comfortable environment.

Acts 16 chronicles a missions trip Timothy took with Paul. Later, Paul described the conditions Timothy was exposed to on that trip.

> We put no stumbling block in anyone's path, so that our ministry would not be discredited. Rather, as servants of God, we commend ourselves in every way: in great endurance; in troubles, hardships and distresses; in beatings, imprisonments and riots; in hard work, sleepless nights and hunger; in purity, understanding, patience and kindness; . . . through glory and dishonor, bad report and good report; genuine, yet regarded as impostors; known, yet regarded as unknown; dying, and yet we live on; beaten, and yet not killed; sorrowful, yet always rejoicing; poor, yet making many rich; having nothing, and yet possessing everything (2 Corinthians 6:3–10).

A mission for Christ is a journey that takes our teen out of her comfortable surroundings and puts her in situations that require a great deal of sacrifice.

Teens who never make any sacrifices for Christ, never get to taste the fruit of such a lifestyle. Christ said, "Whoever finds his life will lose it, and whoever loses his life for my sake will find it" (Matthew 10:39).

In normal home, school, and church environments, our teen rarely has to make any real sacrifices for Jesus Christ. A missions trip, planned correctly, requires our teen to move out of her safety zone and make sacrifices she's never been asked to make before.

Spring break in dusty Mexico

During spring break one year, a team of high schoolers went to Mexico for a ten-day missions trip. The teens slept every night in a compound. It was very hot. Dust "twisters" continually swept through camp, covering everything with dirt.

From 8:00 A.M. to 8:00 P.M. each day, the kids worked in a small Mexican village which had no modern bathroom facilities. The kids taught Bible clubs and led various recreational activities.

For a while, it looked as if the kids might lose heart and ask to leave before the ten days were over. However, as soon as they got past the idea that they had to constantly be clean (that took about three days), they really started enjoying it. After ten days, the kids didn't want to go home.

It may be hard to believe, but the experiences that mean the most to our teen are the ones that require the greatest personal sacrifices. Activities or experiences that require little of her will never mean much to her.

If our teen's experiences with Christianity never require her to stretch or sacrifice, Christianity will never mean much to her either.

Many kids look back at their high school years and value most their athletic experiences because of the sacrifices their coaches required of them. Sports are often the only activity during adolescence that requires them to make sacrifices.

Too often, our teens go through adolescence without having to sacrifice as much for Christ as they would for basketball or cheerleading. Involving our kid in a mission for Christ that takes her out of her comfort zone ensures that this won't happen.

Element #3: *Opposition*

On every trip Timothy took with Paul, he experienced persecution for sharing his faith. If we take our teen on a missions trip, she will usually encounter opposition, in one form or another, to what she is trying to accomplish.

The great chase

One group of high school students decided to share Christ on Saturday night in the center of a fairly large town— only to be met with incredible opposition.

The kids in that town literally chased them off the streets and onto their bus by throwing stones at them!

The Christian kids grieved over how lost and blind their attackers were, but they also rejoiced that they actually had an opportunity to suffer for Christ. None of those kids ever forgot that experience.

It's on missions trips that most Christian kids get their first opportunity to experience persecution for their faith. Most Christian teens will only begin to share Christ with others when they're a part of a family or team or group that brings them along to do it.

Timothy was with Paul and Silas and their whole team when he had his first experiences of sharing his faith and encountering persecution.

The value of missions trips

Missions trips expose what's inside our hearts

Missions for Jesus Christ are an ideal context for exposing what's going on inside of people. Paul told Timothy, "You know all about my teaching. You know all about my way of life, my heart, my sufferings" (2 Timothy 3:10).

How did Timothy know all these things? How did he know what Paul was like on the inside? He went with him on several missions trips for Christ. Missions trips thrust people together twenty-four hours a day, suffering and serving side by side. People really get to see what's inside each other.

If Jesus Christ is inside, we see that. If he's not, well, look what Paul found out about Demas on a missions trip. "Do your best to come to me, [Timothy,] for Demas, because he loved this world, has deserted me and has gone to Thessalonica" (2 Timothy 4:9).

Missions trips often force us to wrestle with our own hearts. "Why am I having such a hard time caring? Why am I always grouchy? Why do I let everybody else do the hard work?" We learn a lot about ourselves. We learn how far our hearts are from being the person God uses to accomplish His work. Missions trips should never be used to develop spiritual pride but to expose spiritual poverty.

Around home and church, we can hide spiritual poverty for a long time. We can have no vital relationship with Christ and still fool ourselves and others into believing we are strong spiritual examples. Any of us can pretend to be spiritual for an hour or two a week.

Missions trips expose the real condition of our hearts and require us to do things that only hearts in tune with Jesus Christ can do.

Tad's trip goes to the dog

On a missions trip, Tad, his wife, and his kids were assigned to sleep at the home of one of the families in the church that his team was helping.

As Tad walked into the front room of this house the first night, he noticed the living room couch had been made into a bed. A big, hairy, slobbering dog lay on the sheets with his head on the pillow.

Tad did a double take, and the hostess shouted at the dog, "Get down from there! Get down!" Then she added, "He's been doing that all day!"

That night, just as Tad feared, he was assigned to sleep on that couch.

When Tad arrived at the church the next day, the other families were talking about their stay in a fabulous mansion where they had their own suite with a jacuzzi tub and a swimming pool. "Why do they always get better accommodations than we do?" Tad muttered under his breath. "When we get to the next church, I'm going to make the housing assignments myself and make sure that . . ." Tad caught himself.

His heart was exposed. He had to ask himself, "Am I on this trip to serve the interests of Christ, or to get something for myself?"

We find out on missions trips, too, that the real spiritual leaders are not necessarily those who appeared to be the leaders on the first day of the trip. The most talented are not usually the spiritual leaders either. Often the "stars" think they should be excused from ordinary labor.

Kids who are the celebrities at school, the best looking, the smartest, the most talented, often can't keep up with the ordinary kids, who wouldn't have been pegged as spiritual leaders back at church.

On missions trips, our teen will discover that her usefulness to Christ has nothing to do with talent and good looks. It has everything to do with what's in her heart.

Often, the kids on missions trips who have the best hearts are the kids who look the plainest, the most ordinary. No one would ever think about asking them to get up and speak in chapel or bring the sermon on Youth Sunday. They might stutter. No one would ever think about electing them to the youth cabinet. They don't seem that creative.

Yet, when we get these kids out on a missions trip, we discover what they're made of. They're the ones we want around when there's dirty work to be done. They're the ones we want to encourage to pursue Christian ministry as a career.

Seeing our teen in action on missions trips gives us our best context for discovering true spiritual needs and true spiritual leadership.

Missions trips expose who Christ really is

Missions trips for Jesus Christ are also an ideal context for experiencing the presence and the power of God.

After becoming a Christian, if Paul had stayed safely at home, studying the Scriptures and fellowshiping with other Christians, instead of traveling on missions for Christ, he would have missed the most profound experiences of the power and presence of Jesus Christ.

When our teen lives her life in comfortable surroundings, she doesn't see much evidence of Christ's power and protection in her life because she's not doing anything that needs God's help. The demands of missions trips require her to depend on Christ for strength and protection.

Paul described one of these experiences to Timothy. "At my first defense, no one came to my support, but everyone deserted me. May it not be held against them. But the Lord stood at my side and gave me strength" (2 Timothy 4:16).

Think of it! As Paul stood before the Caesar we read about in history books, he actually experienced Jesus Christ standing by his side, giving him strength. This was an experience Paul would never have had if he had not taken the risk to boldly speak out for Christ on a missions trip.

Paul went on to say, "I was delivered from the lion's mouth. The Lord will rescue me from every evil attack" (2 Timothy 4:17–18).

Wow! To expose our teen to that kind of power should be the desire of every parent! Once our kid witnesses the power and presence of Christ in her life, she will have little reason to walk away from it.

Most of the time, when a teen walks away from Christianity, it's because she's never tasted the power or the presence of Jesus Christ. To her, Jesus is no more real than Santa Claus. She's heard people talk about Santa, but she's never personally experienced his power or his presence in her life.

Missions trips capture a teenager's imagination and affection

Remember how Christ's disciples reacted after their first missionary journey? They had great joy and excitement for they had seen Jesus' power in action! It captured their imaginations.

As parents, we'll never capture our teen's heart for Christ until we've first filled her imagination with what Jesus Christ can do. When she starts to see Jesus' power, she asks herself, "What could Christ do through me if I gave my whole life to Him?"

Have you ever been to a Student Congress? It's quite a show! High school students from around each state gather for days at a time, debating current political topics and laws.

They elect their own governor (president at national events) and write and pass their own legislation. The sense of power and prestige captures the kids' imaginations, and many of them choose to go into law and politics.

Cheerleading competitions and their nonstop enthusiasm also capture a teen's imagination. But where's that going to take our teen? Other teens get involved in hobbies, participate in fairs and expositions. Other students get wrapped up in social causes that capture their imaginations. They feel power, especially when they get a taste of how their involvement in such causes actually makes a difference in the world. Many of these students invest their whole lives in these same causes.

Whatever captures our teenager's imagination during adolescence is usually what she will give her life to. Missions trips give our teen an opportunity to imagine what it would be like to live her life for Jesus Christ. This is a vital step in guiding a teenager to a faith that lasts.

If you take an informal survey of Christian men and women who have given their lives to serving Christ and ask them "What first excited you about serving Jesus Christ?" almost without exception they'll tell you about a missions trip during adolescence when they saw Jesus Christ transform people's lives.

Planning a family missions trip

Effective missions trips, especially ones involving our teen, require careful planning. We must avoid the temptation to throw something together haphazardly.

Assess your ministry gifts

What skills do our family members have? How could we serve others? What kind of maturity and experience do we have?

If our family is still young and inexperienced in missions, maybe our first trip shouldn't center around evangelism as much as manual labor or relief. Visiting the elderly, working with children, or feeding the poor could be places to start.

Much depends on what our family has to offer. There might be a doctor, nurse, someone with construction skills, artist, or computer whiz among us. Maybe a family member gardens or farms. Maybe we know how to paint a house or do some other kind of handiwork that could assist a ministry.

Look and pray for opportunities one or two rungs above the family's maturity and comfort level

Don't look for something ten rungs above it or a few rungs below it. If our family knows how to rough it, we can look for more primitive, stretching destinations.

If our family's idea of roughing it is staying at Best Western, then our first missions trip could be to a church here in the United States. That would be a place to start.

It's important not to think of a missions trip as a one-time event, but rather a family tradition. Each year, as our family matures, the trips can be progressively more challenging.

Investigate opportunities to harness existing family interests, burdens, or associations

Maybe, through our church, we've met some missionaries or representatives of missions organizations that told us of their needs. Many Christian ministries in the United States— both inner city and rural—could use our help. A number of camps need volunteers, too, especially during the summer.

Christian organizations welcome volunteers—particularly when a whole family is willing to come and work together.

Determine the budget and support needed

Before we count a missions trip out because we can't afford it, we need to do a firm cost analysis.

Generally, missions trips are cheaper than vacations. And because it's a missions endeavor, our family can learn a lot about how God supplies resources through friends and family who may help with financial support.

Together, around the kitchen or dining room table, we can work out a missions budget, and pray for God to provide the needed support. Then we can write letters to friends and family, explaining the project as a mission for Christ and inviting their support through both prayer and finances.

Explore the possibility of two or three families going together as a team

It could be very exciting and rewarding to invite other families, especially single-parent families whose kids know each other, to join together in a missions endeavor.

The ministry gifts of one family could complement the other's quite effectively. But the two families would want to meet together weekly as a team—praying, planning, and preparing for the trip.

Spend a minimum of three months preparing

Much of the value of a missions trip is in the preparation and planning. During this time, every family member needs to have a job, assignment, or role that stretches that person one or two rungs.

As a family, we need to make sure we discuss thoroughly our itinerary and proposed activities.

A big part of the experience is talking together about how we want to serve Christ. The more we get our teens to participate in the planning, the more they'll "own" the trip.

If our trip will take us into a different culture, we'll need someone to give our family an orientation to that culture. Maybe, as a team, we can work out some songs, skits, or children's programs to do together. It's also a good idea to assemble some "care packages" to take along.

We need to make sure, however, that our preparation emphasizes the inner person, getting our hearts ready to serve. We will want to study the Bible together, reflecting on the kind of person God uses to accomplish His work.

At the end of the trip, we also need to build in evaluation and debriefing time. That may mean meeting at least once a week for several weeks after the trip is over, talking about what we learned and how we're going to use it now that we're back home.

Permanent partners in missions with our teen

On a missions trip there's a good chance our whole family will catch a vision for serving Christ together. There are a number of continuing ministries right in our own community that we could come back and do together.

Home Bible studies for our friends—both our teen's friends and our own. Lead it together!

A family-taught Sunday school class (in any area from the nursery through juniors). Our whole family could take this on as a project, each family member having a role.

Backyard Bible clubs. This is a natural family opportunity because we can reach our own neighborhood.

Nursing homes, orphanages, or rescue missions. We can make it a holiday tradition to serve together on Thanksgiving or Christmas Day.

New families at church. Adopt them into the church family and you make some new friends at the same time!

Pitfalls to avoid

Just as Paul used missions trips to capture Timothy's imagination and affection for Christ, we can do the same for our teen. We don't have to wait for other people to plan them for her. We can plan them ourselves. When we do, it's important to avoid some common pitfalls.

Don't make missions trips performance trips
Families that are highly talented can be tempted to turn

missions trips into concert tours. Remember, missions trips should take our family outside our comfort zones, requiring us to depend on God for the necessary skills and resources.

Missions trips that revolve around public performances tend to make us celebrities instead of servants. They also tend to distance us from the people we're serving, making it difficult for us to actually see Christ at work in their lives.

Avoid spectator-orientated trips

True missions trips make each member of our family an active participant in accomplishing a task or project for Christ. Teenagers become merely spectators if we take them to Christian camps, conventions, or music festivals as a missions trip.

Don't make missions trips glamorous or "resortish"

One youth group took a mission trip aboard a commercial cruise ship, sending the kids ashore at seven different ports where they stood on a corner for a few hours passing out New Testaments. The trip was carefully planned so the kids didn't miss any shopping trips or suntan sessions. This group was using a missions trip as an excuse to take a vacation.

For a missions trip to be most effective, we should live with or live like the people we're helping. It should involve us and our teen in "little incarnations" in which we become servants to others.

Don't overprogram

The schedule on a missions trip should be flexible enough to allow for two things: *seizing unpredictable opportunities* to serve Christ and *time to be with the people we're serving*. We don't want such a tight schedule that our teens miss opportunities to build relationships with people and observe how God's working in their lives.

Don't make missions trips too brief

When it comes to missions trips, the longer, the better. One-week hit-and-run trips are limited in their effectiveness. It usually takes about a week for us to adjust to a new culture and be weaned from all our comforts. That's when we can start enjoying what it means to serve others in another culture.

Also, it usually takes several days to build the kind of relationships with others that give a glimpse of how God is working in their lives.

The highs and lows of missions trips

Not every mission trip turns out as expected. Every trip is sure to have its highs and lows. But opportunities to learn and teach come in the low moments as well as the high ones.

Dakota missions trip

Immediately after graduating from seminary, Lyle invited his best friend, Wesley, to join him on a missions trip. Lyle was the pastor of a church in South Dakota, and one of the church's ministries was to sponsor and help staff a camp each summer.

"What would you think, Wes, about coming out to South Dakota and the two of us working as a team to help this camp for teen weeks?" Lyle asked.

Wesley agreed.

The two of them brought a lot of energy and enthusiasm to the camp, and the Lord used them to win many kids to Christ.

The next year, Lyle and Wesley, along with their wives, decided to make this Dakota missions trip an annual event, which they soon nicknamed "Black Hills Week."

Every year the couples—and later their children—performed a myriad of tasks. No job was too small or too big for the two families.

When Wesley's oldest child was between eighth and ninth grades, she led two junior high kids to Christ and followed up with them via mail. Each week she sent them Bible study materials and monitored their spiritual progress.

The following summer, Wesley's daughter brought a friend with her to camp—as did the other two girls she had led to Christ. What a reunion it was! That week each of their friends also accepted Christ.

Black Hills Week became a "must" every year for both families.

Then, the trip that had thrilled both families and produced so many changed lives, suddenly ended in a way no one could have predicted.

One year Lyle had a stroke the day before camp. Wesley's family arrived to find Lyle comatose and given no hope to live.

Both families were shattered as they met in Lyle's hospital room. It was next to impossible to concentrate on Black Hills Week when Lyle was close to death. The members of the family—usually together in such a happy way at this time for years—joined hands to pray.

Suddenly, like something out of a mystery, Lyle sat straight up. His wife ran to him. Lyle looked around the room, and then gently spoke, "I knew you'd come."

Wesley moved to the bed.

Lyle looked at him and said, "Do you know Psalm 23?"

His wife and Wesley both answered yes.

"You know where it says, 'I shall not want'?"

Again, yes.

"It's true, you know," Lyle said. "He takes care of everything, and He's taking care of me."

Everyone listened in stunned silence. Then he spoke once more.

"I'm glad you came. I knew you would." With that he lay back down and stopped breathing! His life was over.

What had been, for a day, the worst Black Hills Week—filled with fear and sadness—suddenly changed.

After the funeral services were over, the two families went to the last two days of camp.

Their missions trip was different this year. They told the kids at camp what they'd seen. The relationships they'd developed by serving Christ together had given them an opportunity to see Christ himself in the face of their friend and leader.

On missions trips, always plan for the unexpected. Plan on our families getting a glimpse of Christ in the most unexpected but powerful ways. When it happens, none of us will ever be the same.

Nine

Teaching Our Teen How to Use the Bible

One of the most effective techniques of authors, film directors, and scriptwriters is the "secret weapon."

The villain in the sword fight steadily and systematically gains an advantage over the hero. However, just as the villain is about to win the duel, the hero flips his sword from his right hand to his left and announces, "I have a surprise for you. *I'm not right-handed!*"

A pack of wolves is attacking a defenseless pair of cubs. The cubs go deeper and deeper into their cave to escape the pack's bold charges. Up against the back wall of the cave, the cubs can hold the wolf pack at bay no longer. Just as all seems hopeless, suddenly, out of the shadows, rising like a mountain, appears the mother grizzly—*twelve feet tall, all teeth, and snarling mad!*

A handful of outnumbered patriots makes a valiant last stand against an invading army of hundreds. For days, they resist by their courage and wits. But now they're running out of time, supplies, and space. They're about to be overrun when *a bugle sounds and reinforcements of hundreds of fresh troops come rushing down the mountainside to their rescue!*

According to Paul, we have a powerful secret weapon for guiding our teens to a faith that lasts. However, unlike secret weapons in the movies, it shouldn't be used as a last resort, called in when all hope is gone and all else has failed. Instead, it should be a powerful part of our strategy in parenting our teen from the very beginning.

Our secret weapon in guiding our teen to a faith that lasts is *the Bible.* In his last letter to Timothy, Paul described how he used the Bible to nurture and shape his spiritual son's faith.

> Continue in what you have learned and have become convinced of, because you know those from whom you learned it, and how from infancy you have known the holy Scriptures, which are able to make you wise for salvation through faith in Christ Jesus. All Scripture is God-breathed and is useful for teaching, rebuking, correcting and training in righteousness, so that the man of God may be thoroughly equipped for every good work (2 Timothy 3:14–17).

Paul was not content merely to use the Bible as a tool in Timothy's life. He also taught Timothy practical ways of using Scripture to strengthen his own faith.

If we don't use the secret weapon, it remains a secret

Many times, we as parents don't have the foggiest idea how to teach our kids practical ways to use the Bible because we don't know how to use it ourselves. As a result, when we're struggling with how to get our teen to follow Christ, our most powerful weapon remains unused.

It sits on the shelf except when we carry it to church on Sunday. The Bible is not something we use through the week. Our secret weapon remains a secret.

Why our teens don't use the Bible

Because the Bible is so often misused or underused around teens, they often come to wrong, destructive conclusions about it.

Teens may view the Bible as a club
Some kids view the Bible as an instrument of torture we adults wield to get them to do what they don't want to do. Many times, this is the only way kids ever see the Bible used. We bring it out and club them over the head with its teachings.

"Dad makes me cringe"
Hal, a father of three teenagers, took each of his kids out to breakfast or lunch once each week. He found this to be the best way to get a little time alone with each of them to talk about what was going on in their lives and occasionally to do a little Bible study with them.

But Hal began to notice that his kids cringed or rolled their eyes whenever he brought the Bible along on one of these meals. One day, he decided to ask his daughter about it.

She got right to the point, "Whenever you bring that Bible along, I always know what's coming. A sermon! And it's usually because I'm in trouble about something."

Hal thought his kids didn't like his bringing the Bible because they were embarrassed. But his daughter's comments helped him see that wasn't the issue at all.

Later on, Hal's son echoed the same sentiments. "It's like a club that you use, Dad. Whenever we kids are doing something wrong, you pull out the Bible to get us back in line."

Inadvertently, Hal was giving his kids a wrong impression about the Bible. They didn't see the Bible as useful or practical—only as intimidating and shaming.

Teens may see the Bible as a collection of old stories

Many teens feel that Bible stories are out of date and irrelevant to their lives.

A new Christian's praise

Shortly after Troy became a Christian, his pastor asked him to sing a song with a biblical message for the Sunday morning worship service.

Troy was a college student who had been a singer in a rock band when he came to Christ, and his pastor was eager to see him put his musical talent to work for God.

Troy racked his brain to decide what to sing. He didn't know any Christian songs, but he loved music recorded by Elvis Presley. As he was reviewing his Presley songs, Troy came across one that at least mentioned a story from the Bible. Although only one line referred to Samson and Delilah, Troy decided it was the only song with a biblical message in his whole repertoire.

When Sunday arrived, Troy stepped to the microphone with his guitar to open the service. Putting his whole heart into it, Troy crooned the Elvis Presley rendition of "Hard Headed Woman" to the stunned congregation.

Troy's pastor learned an important lesson that day. Like Troy, many teens view the Bible as nothing more than a collection of old stories. These stories are kind of fun to hear but not relevant to their lives at all. A Bible message, they assume, is nothing more than a recitation of one of the same stories they've heard a hundred times before.

Teens may view the Bible as a book they can't understand

Often teens who have just become Christians will decide to start in Genesis and read the Bible through from cover to cover.

They usually make it to somewhere in the book of Leviticus. Then they give up because they don't understand what they're reading.

Although the Bible is an immensely useful and practical tool for everyone, especially teenagers, it is not easily mastered or understood without a guide.

When we guide our teen to portions of the Bible that are more easily understood and applied to his life, he begins to develop a biblical literacy which will eventually equip him to use and enjoy the whole Bible.

Teens may view the Bible as God telling them they can't have a relationship with Him

Some kids come to church and what they think they hear from the Bible is God saying, "This is why I don't want anything to do with you. You don't measure up!"

So, they drop out and say, "I'll come back when I get my life together."

It's understandable that, without help, kids can mistake the true message of the Bible for a distorted version. The real message of the Bible is this: "God can only have the relationship He wants with us through His son, Jesus Christ."

In a lot of ways the Bible is not a user-friendly book. On every page it exposes things in our hearts that keep us from experiencing the life God created us to enjoy. But on every page it also gives us hope by showing us where we can go to get our hearts changed or made new.

As parents and Bible teachers, it's easy to portray the Bible to our teen as lists of rules or steps he's supposed to use to change his heart. But the Bible invites our kid into a personal relationship with Christ, not a personal-improvement program.

Teens may view the Bible as a magical book

Some kids believe that the act of reading the Bible in itself will make them spiritual.

Quiz team's night out

Many churches encourage their teenagers to become involved in Bible quizzing.

One year, the team from one church memorized the whole book of Romans. The kids knew this book so well they could finish any verse, word for word, if the quiz master called out the chapter and verse numbers.

After winning the district championships that year, the team traveled by van to the nationals in Florida.

On the way there, the team stayed overnight at another church. After the adult leaders fell asleep, some of the team members snuck out of the church and vandalized the neighborhood, tearing down mailboxes, damaging cars, and spray-painting some property.

These were the same kids who had just spent the year memorizing and studying the book of Romans!

It's a good lesson for every parent. Just getting our kid reading the Bible as an activity doesn't necessarily change him on the inside. The key to helping our kid grow spiritually isn't getting him into the Bible. It's getting the Bible into him, teaching him how to let the Bible control and shape the way he thinks and acts!

If we give our kid the impression that just reading or studying the Bible will somehow mysteriously or magically change him, then all we do is make him superstitious, not genuinely spiritual. He may begin to view the Bible as a good-luck charm, thinking that just carrying it around and doing some magic ritual with it automatically will change him.

Other kids believe that by reading the Bible they rack up brownie points with God.

Bulimia and the Bible

Sharon, a high school junior, used to feel so guilty about her bulimic behavior that every time she threw up her food she would go read the Bible for hours in order to feel better. She believed that reading the Bible magically took away her sin.

Two truths about the Bible's origin and purpose that every teen should know

The Bible is unique, the most powerful book ever written. Yet, too often, we underestimate it. We undervalue it. Around our teens, we even undersell it.

How can we correct this tendency? By making sure our teen understands two great truths that make the Bible unique and powerful.

As Paul reminded Timothy of the importance of the Word of God in becoming the person God wanted him to be, he emphasized two important truths about the Bible that every teenager needs to know.

Truth #1: *The origin of the Bible is different than any other book our teen will ever read.*

Paul reminded Timothy about the Bible's unique origin when he wrote, "All Scripture is God-breathed" (2 Timothy 3:16).

The origin of the Bible is God. God created the truths of the Bible. They are an expression of who He is. Through the human beings who wrote the Bible, God breathed the message he wanted us to have.

Our teen is confronted regularly with questions that challenge the Bible's origin: How do you know that God really wrote the Bible? How do we know for sure that the Bible Jesus endorsed is the same Bible we have today?

We must not be afraid of our kids asking the hard questions. We as parents should get down in the trenches with our teen and search *with him* to find the answers.

Father and son get in the trenches

Dwight was a construction worker whose oldest son was always asking intriguing questions. One day, the boy confronted his dad with a series of questions about inaccuracies in the Bible.

"Dad, I've got a friend who says there are some mistakes in the Bible. He says that there are even typographical errors in it. He proved it to me—in my own Bible!"

Dwight didn't like the feel of the situation, but he didn't panic or come down hard on his son. Instead, he took it as a challenge. "How about our looking at it together?" he said.

They both enrolled in a Bible correspondence course on the history of the Bible. They checked out magazines from the library. They read other books on the subject.

Over a period of nearly six months this father and son actively pursued an adventure that didn't involve sports, cars, fishing, or hobbies.

At a nearby Christian college they talked to experts on the history of the Bible. They discussed it at great length with their pastor. Several men and women in the church got involved in their odyssey.

As they explored, they found that there had been a few translation mistakes over the centuries. However, it soon became obvious that the integrity of the Bible was nothing short of miraculous.

They read the challenges of the anthropologists, linguists, and archaeologists and learned to respect them. But, they also learned that the same experts, throughout the years, had been proven wrong—again and again—when they challenged the Bible.

There were some challenges Dwight and his son couldn't refute, but they came to the conclusion that a hundred years from now more discoveries will have cleared up those questions. And, of course, by then they would be in heaven—with all their questions answered.

They studied great doubters in history, such as evolution proponent Charles Darwin, and Ben Hur author Lew Wallace, who eventually believed in the authenticity of the Bible, just by studying it for themselves.

The result? This father and son's faith grew. They had an adventure neither could have ever planned or bought. They grew to appreciate each other and grew in their faith as they more fully understood that the Bible came from God.

Truth #2: *The purpose of the Bible is to deepen our relationship with Christ.*

At first, the Bible introduced Timothy to Christ and helped him begin his journey of faith with Christ. Paul reminded Timothy, "From infancy you have known the holy Scriptures, which are able to make you wise for salvation through faith in Christ Jesus" (2 Timothy 3:15).

But, after accomplishing this goal, the Bible didn't lose its usefulness. Paul emphasized the ongoing purpose of the Bible in Timothy's life. "All scripture is . . . useful . . . so that the man of God may be thoroughly equipped for every good work" (2 Timothy 3:16–17).

Paul taught Timothy how to use the Bible as a tool to continue growing in his faith and love for Christ. Most teenagers don't understand how to use the Bible this way unless they have an opportunity to observe their parents putting the Bible to practical use.

The Bible describes itself as a sword or scalpel used to expose the things in our hearts that hurt our relationship with Christ and destroy our ability to do His work. "For the word of God is living and active. Sharper than any double-edged sword, it penetrates even to dividing soul and spirit, joints and marrow; it judges the thoughts and attitudes of the heart" (Hebrews 4:12).

To model for teens how to use the Bible in this way, we must first understand what it is in our hearts that opposes Christ.

Understanding what's in our own hearts

The heart we're referring to, of course, is not the muscle in our chest that pumps blood. It's our soul—the immaterial part of us that thinks and chooses and controls our behavior.

At the core: a thirst only God can quench

God has created every one of us with a thirsty heart. We thirst for something that will give us life. In John 7:37–38 Christ offers to quench that thirst. "If anyone is thirsty, let him come to me and drink. Whoever believes in me . . . streams of living water will flow from within him."

In spite of Jesus' promise, we all end up looking for ways to quench our thirst apart from Him. Any relief we find for our inner thirst apart from Christ is only temporary, yet there's something in our hearts that keeps making us try anyway.

It's as if there's a corrupt government in our hearts, resisting Christ and ordering us to go elsewhere to satisfy our thirst.

The corrupt government in our hearts

We might imagine our heart to be a country stricken by drought. A cry rises throughout the land for relief. Christ stands ready to bring showers of refreshment. All He needs is an invitation.

As the cries reach our heart's government, it quickly dispatches the problem to a series of departments, looking for a solution. But each of these departments has been corrupted by a conspiracy within the government to keep Christ out of the way, to keep Him from getting control of our heart.

The department of misjustice (D.O.M.)

This department decides who is to blame for our heart's drought. It approaches the problem with a set of assumptions that prejudices its deliberations from the beginning.

First, the D.O.M. assumes that the drought is unfair. Everyone is entitled to a life free from thirst. Therefore, a misjustice has been committed.

Second, the D.O.M. assumes that the drought cannot be the fault of its own government. Somebody else must be to blame. The only logical person to blame is Christ. If He really cared, He wouldn't have let this drought happen. Therefore, He can't be trusted to help with the problem.

Third, the D.O.M. assumes that the world is its best ally in solving the problem—a much better friend than God is! If approached in the proper way, the world can be persuaded to give our thirsty heart everything that will satisfy it. Therefore, we must find a way to become better friends with the world.

When the D.O.M. is finished reviewing the problem, it passes its recommendations along to the next department.

The department of world affairs (D.W.A.)

The D.W.A.'s assignment is to establish a friendship treaty with the world. In order to do this, it must conduct a fact-finding mission.

First, it has to locate something in the world that will take care of our thirst. It begins to explore every possible relationship we have, looking for some source of satisfaction.

Eventually, the D.W.A. identifies one or more relationships as the best potential sources, which it then designates as "priority relationships."

After the D.W.A. investigates each of our priority relationships to determine what we have to give in each in order to get what we want, the D.W.A. turns to its last task, creating a new identity for us.

The D.W.A. calculates what kind of person we must be to control the world's resources. It may decide that we have to masquerade at all times as a winner in order to capture the world's respect and affection. Or it may decide that masquerading as a total loser would be more advantageous because of the sympathy it could capture.

The D.W.A. has hundreds of identities to choose from. Once it decides which is best, it sends a "work order" to a third department.

The department of public works (D.P.W.)

Finding a way to satisfy our own thirst is like digging our own well. It's hard work.

Once the D.P.W. receives the findings of the other departments, it sets goals for the work to be done in every one of our relationships. It gets us busy doing the things in the world that are consistent with our new identity.

The D.P.W. also monitors our progress, keeping pressure on us to always be working when we're around others. Its quality control inspectors react with stiff reprimands should we ever reveal our real identity by what we do or say.

When all our government's best efforts inevitably fail to relieve the drought, the cries of our heart grow even louder. But the corrupt government of our heart will still not permit us to turn to Christ. As long as that administration is in power, the resistance to Christ will continue.

Our thirsty heart will never come to Christ for satisfaction until its corrupt government topples. God's Word, the Bible, is the tool God has given us to attack and overturn that regime. Without it, we are weaponless in the battle to free our own hearts from the tyranny of sin.

Using the Bible to free our hearts

Paul taught Timothy four strategic ways to use the Bible to topple the corrupt government of the heart. He wrote, "All Scripture . . . is profitable for teaching, for reproof, for correction, and for training in righteousness" (2 Timothy 3:16 NAS).

When we don't use the Bible in these ways in our lives, we are not free to do Christ's work. We are bound to do the work of a government unfriendly to Christ.

It would be unthinkable to neglect teaching and modeling for our teens these strategic ways to use the Bible.

For instruction—using the Bible to challenge our faulty assumptions

Paul told Timothy that God gave us the Bible for teaching or instruction. King David of the Old Testament observed that God wants to replace the false beliefs of our heart with liberating truth. "Surely you desire truth in the inner parts; you teach me wisdom in the inmost place" (Psalm 51:6).

King David's son, Solomon, known for his great wisdom, observed why each of our kids needs to apply the Bible to his heart. "Folly is bound up in the heart of a child, but the rod of discipline will drive it far from him" (Proverbs 22:15).

Our rod of discipline is to help our teen honestly explore his heart's automatic assumptions about thirst, God, and the world—in the light of what the Bible says. Used properly, the Bible disrupts the corrupt government in our teen's heart and the false assumptions it makes.

Imagine how the Bible challenges the belief that we deserve more out of life than we're getting. Our world reinforces this belief, but every page in the Word of God radically contradicts it. The Bible tells us that we deserve hell. God's grace, not the world's, keeps us from receiving the judgment we deserve.

Most teens—especially those victimized by divorce, abuse, or serious illness—believe that God has failed them.

A man in the Bible named Job believed this too. After suffering catastrophic losses of his family, wealth, and health, Job accused God of failing him. Through face-to-face instruction, God demolished Job's false beliefs about Him.

When we encourage our teenager to bring his questions about God directly to the Bible, God has the opportunity to instruct our teen as He did Job. Regular exposure to God's Word challenges our teen's faulty beliefs and convinces him that God is someone he can trust.

For reproof—using the Bible to expose our true identity

We live in a world which is almost devoid of honest feedback. This is especially true for our teen. His friends, his teachers, even his family seldom level with him.

The Bible gives us our only reliable glimpse of what kind of people we really are, what kind of selfish interests govern us, how we're using our relationships to satisfy our own thirsts.

The Bible is a mirror that exposes what's in our hearts.

James, Jesus' brother, wrote a letter urging people to take seriously the personal reproof they receive from the Bible. He writes, "Do not merely listen to the word, and so deceive yourselves. Do [something about] what it says. Anyone who listens to the word but does not do [anything about] what it says is like a man who looks at his face in a mirror and, after looking at himself, goes away and immediately forgets what he looks like" (James 1:22–24).

When we use the Bible to reprove and expose who we are, it leaves us looking for help to change. For this we can turn to the Bible again.

For correction—using the Bible to change our direction

Correction was a medical term in Paul's day, used in reference to setting a broken bone. It was the process of taking something that was twisted in the wrong direction and pointing it back in the right direction.

The Bible serves as a road sign that points us and our kids away from exploiting people and into a dependent relationship with Christ. Peter wrote, "Therefore, rid yourselves of all malice and all deceit, hypocrisy, envy, and slander of every kind. Like newborn babies, crave pure spiritual milk, so that by it you may grow up in your salvation, now that you have tasted that the Lord is good" (1 Peter 2:1–3).

Since the natural tendency of our hearts is to draw from others what we can only truly draw from Christ, we constantly need the correction and redirection the Bible provides.

For training in righteousness—using the Bible to measure our progress

God never intended for us to try to change our heart by following the Bible's prescription for righteous behaviors. Only personal, life-changing encounters with Christ can do that!

However, as our hearts are made new by Christ, they must be trained how to walk, just as a new baby must be. The Bible teaches us how to walk by showing us the kinds of behaviors a transformed heart chooses.

The Bible acts as a gauge, measuring how trainable our hearts are. An untrained heart (one that doesn't choose biblical behaviors) is a heart that is still in need of Christ's transforming touch. Paul said, "The law was put in charge to lead us to Christ" (Galatians 3:24).

Showing our teen how to use the Bible in these four ways creates a holy kind of disruption and movement in his life. For this we must be prepared. The Bible is potent. Used properly, it serves as a catalyst that unleashes a chain reaction in the human soul.

How the Bible disrupts our lives

The Bible distresses us

When we and our teen use the Bible as a tool for instruction, reproof, correction, and training, it inevitably raises the level of distress we have about our own lives.

We shouldn't study or teach the Bible just to make us feel good. That would be like trying to use a dentist's drill to induce euphoria. That's not the purpose of a dentist's drill. Nor is it the purpose of the Bible.

Applying the Bible is often a disrupting experience, especially for our teen. Since he is developing adult thinking capacities, any honest encounter with the truths of the Bible will cause him some distress. For this reason, our kid may become mesmerized and spellbound by the Bible, or its haunting nature may make him avoid it.

The Bible makes us want to change our relationship with Christ

The distress the Bible causes us always creates movement either toward Christ or away from Christ, depending on whether we want Him to change our heart or leave us alone.

The Bible, used properly, makes it impossible to stay lukewarm toward Christ. We become either hot or cold. Neutrality isn't an option.

As parents, we must understand that any movement the Bible creates in our kid's life is always better than no movement at all. If our teen moves away from Christ, we can openly deal with him as a drifter.

The Bible causes us to change how we relate to others

The distress and movement the Bible creates in our lives eventually affects our relationships. Our behavior toward others becomes more loving if our movement is toward Christ or more destructive if our movement is away from Christ. Bible study that does not significantly affect our relationships lacks true instruction, reproof, correction, and training in righteousness.

It's important to encourage our teen to attend Bible studies and Sunday school classes. But we must pray that the Lord will use these studies or classes to shake up our teen by increasing his distress about himself, motivating him to move toward Christ, and altering the way he relates to others. These are the same goals we should have in family Bible studies, too.

The Bible does not allow us to hold false beliefs about God or about ourselves. Scripture is the most powerful tool we can use to guide our teen to a faith that lasts. It is our secret weapon.

Making Bible study dynamic for our teenagers

Here are some suggestions for getting our teen involved in a dynamic interaction with the Bible as described above.

Always treat the Bible as a meal to be enjoyed, not a duty to be endured

Perhaps the greatest service to our teen is to impart a love for the Bible by the passion we display toward God's Word. Psalm 119 describes the kind of passion for the Bible that we'd like to see every teenager "catch."

> My soul is consumed with longing for your laws at all times. . . . I run in the path of your commands, for there I find delight. . . . For I delight in your commandments because I love them. . . . If your law had not been my delight, I would have perished in my affliction. . . . I gain understanding from your precepts; therefore I hate every wrong path. . . . I open my mouth and pant, longing for your commands. . . . Streams of tears flow from my eyes, for your law is not obeyed (vv. 20, 32, 47, 92, 104, 131, 136).

A father's passion inspires a classic

The life of one teenager named Frederick was transformed when he observed in his father this kind of passion for the Bible.

Frederick's father had become deathly ill, and in desperation, he turned to God's Word for comfort. The Bible, which he had previously viewed with indifference, suddenly became a book of life and comfort to him.

He asked Frederick to spend every hour he wasn't in school reading the Scriptures to him. Revelation 19:6 quickly became the father's favorite verse, one that he asked young Frederick to read over and over again. "Hallelujah! For our Lord God Almighty reigns!"

Young Frederick—George Frederick Handel—never forgot that verse from the Bible.

Years later, he immortalized Revelation 19:6 in his inspiring classic the "Hallelujah Chorus." His father's passion for the Bible became his own!

Let our teen see us using the Bible to boldly shake up our own lives

This is something we cannot fake, of course. Our teenager always knows when we are pretending. So, we need to come to the Bible with an open heart, allowing it to disrupt us, drive us into a deeper relationship with Christ, and radically alter the way we relate to others. When our teen observes this, the Bible captures his attention and respect. He realizes it is no ordinary book. It's a living book, not to be trifled with.

Remember, we can't force this reaction. The Spirit of God will orchestrate the results as we honestly turn to the Bible for daily self-examination and nourishment. "Man does not live on bread alone," Christ told Satan, "but on every word that comes from the mouth of God" (Matthew 4:4).

When we make our time of reflection on the Bible our most important meal of the day, it will be impossible to keep it a secret from our teenager.

Speak honestly to our teen about how the Bible is shaking up our lives

Imagine the impact of sharing words like the following with a teen at dinner some night:

"Remember when Grandma and Grandpa were here yesterday? I was grouchy with them. You probably noticed. I hardly realized how unloving and ugly I'd been until I caught a glimpse of myself in the book of Ephesians, just before I went to bed last night.

"It was as if Paul had written the words just for me. 'Get rid of all bitterness, rage and anger, brawling and slander, along with every form of malice. Be kind and compassionate to one another, forgiving each other, just as in Christ God forgave you' (Ephesians 4:31–32).

"That's when I realized how bad I am at forgiving. When I told Christ that these verses described my heart and asked Him to replace my anger with love, the first thing I wanted to do was have a long talk with Grandma and Grandpa—something that's long overdue.

"First thing this morning, I called them and went over to talk with them. It was one of the hardest things I ever did, but I'm glad I listened to Christ speaking to me in the Bible."

Hearing us talk about how we have allowed the Bible to shake us up, invites our teen to do the same.

Require our teen, on a regular basis, to hear the Bible taught relevantly in a language he understands

As our teen is making the most important decision of his life—what kind of person he wants to be—he must have regular exposure to relevant and poignant teaching from the Bible.

We are wise when we provide this for our teenager, both inside our home (talking about the Bible around the dinner table) and outside our home (requiring our teen to attend at least one meeting or class a week in which the Bible is taught in a language he understands).

God has gifted certain men and women to uniquely relate the Bible to teenagers. As parents, we need to search out opportunities for our kid to study the Bible with them.

As long as our teen is still in high school, it is appropriate to give him several options for this kind of Bible study and require him to take advantage of at least one a week.

Help our teen avoid situations in which the Bible is taught in toxic ways

The Bible is powerful medicine that can be used in both bad and good ways. We never want to require our teen to attend events at which the Bible is taught in toxic ways.

Bible study is toxic when taught in a lifeless or boring manner without relevant application for our teen at his stage in life. Bible study is toxic when it's given in such large doses that our kid can't possibly digest or apply it. He becomes numb to the truth. Bible study is toxic when it is taught strictly as literature or history without any effort to instruct, reprove, correct, or train a person's heart. And Bible study is toxic when used to intimidate or shame our teen into doing things he doesn't want to do.

When teenagers are victimized by toxic Bible study methods, they become discouraged. Their healthy appetite for God is ruined. Their spiritual vitality is poisoned, and God's words of life are turned into words of death.

When we fail to use our best weapon

In World War II, Germany developed two secret weapons that could have won the war—a superfast twin-jet fighter and a primitive missile.

Professor Willi Messerschmitt, an aviation genius, had developed the *ME–262* twin-jet fighter. The *ME–262* could cruise at 520 miles per hour, which was 120 MPH faster than anything the Allies had. The dominating fighter was ready for production in 1943, a year before D-Day.

If Hitler had used this fighter on D-Day, the Allies wouldn't have had air superiority. Without air superiority, D-Day—the beginning of the end for Germany—would have resulted in total defeat for the Allies.

Likewise, the V-1 missile that Germany possessed but failed to use, would have created havoc for the Allies on the beaches of France during D-Day invasions.

But Hitler, underestimating the strength of his enemy, didn't consider the invasion a serious enough threat to use his two most powerful weapons.

As parents, we must never make the same mistake. Our enemy is formidable, but so is our secret weapon. We must never neglect to usc it in the battle for our teen's faith.

Ten

Strengthening Our Teen
to Stand Alone

"Stand by me" and "lean on me" are popular mottos that have been immortalized in songs, books, and movies. They incorporate wonderful concepts of love, support, and togetherness.

However fuzzy and warm these sentiments might be, they won't always apply when our teenagers are building a faith that lasts.

Our teen can say, "Stand by me" when her faith is challenged, and, as loving, caring parents, we will stand by her. When she goes through dark times, we can say to her "lean on me!" That's only natural because adolescence is a time in which we have many opportunities to provide spiritual direction and support for our teen.

However, at the same time, we must also help her strengthen her own convictions. As she becomes more independent, she will be called upon more and more to stand for Christ alone—without our help.

That's a scary thought, but it is even more frightening when we realize how little loyalty of any kind there is in the world today.

Is loyalty a thing of the past?

We and our teenagers are part of a society notorious for an absence of "brand loyalty." We easily change our allegiances or commitments to products, stores, companies, political parties, or candidates, churches, and even people.

Our teens have many more choices today than we had at their age—choices about purchases, colleges, jobs, travel, careers, places to live. They are used to changing their minds often. It is estimated that, on the average, our kids will change their choice of automobiles, colleges, majors in college, careers, places of residence, and marriage partners three times more often than we did.

Because our teens live in a world with so little loyalty, we must help them strengthen their loyalty to Christ. Loyalty is not only a rare quality in today's world; it is treated as a negative quality. Loyalty in religious or moral contexts is especially maligned. One thing is certain: our teen will be ridiculed frequently because of her commitment to Christ.

Three reasons to make this strengthening a priority

Preparing a person to stand alone is important. Paul urged Timothy to "be strong in the grace that is in Christ Jesus" (2 Timothy 2:1). He then gave three reasons why Timothy (and all of our teenagers) need to be strengthened to stand alone for Christ.

Reason #1: *Our teens will soon be totally separated from parents and spiritual mentors.*

Paul knew that Timothy would not be able to depend on him for spiritual encouragement or direction much longer. Paul's death was near. He was "being poured out like a drink offering, and the time [had] come for [his] departure. [He had] fought the good fight, [he had] finished the race, [he had] kept the faith" (2 Timothy 4:6–7).

As parents of teens, we also know that our kid's separation from us is imminent. Although separation by death may still seem a way off, other kinds of separation are on the horizon.

Our teen will soon be separated from us by *distance* as she goes off to college or an apartment in a different part of the city. As she enters new worlds and meets people we know little about, she'll become more and more separated from us by her experiences. Career and marriage choices will lead to even further *emotional* and *geographic* separations.

Our time and contact with our teen, from the time she first enters adolescence until now, will continue to shrink.

All of this means the same thing for our teen that Paul's impending death meant to Timothy. Soon this young person will have to stand spiritually without the help of her parents or spiritual mentors. For some kids, this separation even occurs during adolescence.

When a strong dad dies

Eva, a high school freshman, lost her father to cancer when she was fourteen. Dave, Eva's father, was a committed Christian who taught history and coached at the local high school. Eva had often heard her father sharing his faith in Christ with his students and fellow teachers—many times at the risk of losing his job.

"It's OK," he would say to his family. "If I lose my job, we'll just live in tents and rough it. God will take care of us."

This strengthened Eva to stand alone for Christ as a high school athlete. On the softball and cross-country teams, she never tried to hide her Christian values and behaviors. When questioned or challenged, her quiet confidence, learned from her father, never feared what would happen if she was loyal to Christ.

Dave had no idea how sudden or total his separation would be from his daughter. Still, he wisely lived his life in such a way that his daughter was strengthened to stand alone for Christ—long before he anticipated she would have to.

This was the way Paul parented Timothy. He used every opportunity to strengthen this young man before they were separated for good.

Reason #2: *Our teens will inevitably be deserted by their Christian friends.*

Paul acknowledged this when he wrote to Timothy, "At my first defense, no one came to my support, but everyone deserted me" (2 Timothy 4:16).

Paul discussed these events, not to get Timothy's sympathy or support, but to teach him where to find the strength to stand alone. "The Lord stood at my side and gave me strength, so that through me the message might be fully proclaimed" (2 Timothy 4:17).

At one time or another, our teen will be deserted by even her closest friends, just as Paul was, and she will certainly need the strength to stand alone.

Carolyn is accused

For Carolyn, this experience first occurred in college. After high school graduation, she attended a state university near her home. Carolyn quickly got involved with a campus fellowship of Christians and became known as one of the strongest Christians on campus.

By her sophomore year, Carolyn was taking an active role in promoting outreach events and dorm Bible studies on campus.

She was a gentle but firm defender of Christianity in her classes when professors or students tried to attribute all the ills of the world to Christian teachings or influences. And Carolyn enjoyed the support of dozens of other Christians active in the campus fellowship.

That all changed, however, when one of her professors accused her of plagiarism. Although Carolyn denied doing anything wrong, word quickly spread through the department that Carolyn was a cheat and a fake.

Sadly, most of her Christian friends, without even giving Carolyn a chance to clear her name, wrote her off and began avoiding her.

At the same time to make matters worse, Carolyn received word that her parents were getting a divorce. In her time of greatest need, Carolyn found that nearly all her Christian friends had deserted her.

Carolyn had to wait three excruciating months before the investigators dropped the unjust charges. During those three months, Carolyn literally stood alone with Christ. She learned what it meant to hold onto her faith without the support of other Christians.

As an upperclassman, Carolyn saw many of her unsaved friends and classmates come to Christ. Some told her the reason they listened to her was because they had seen the way she weathered her parents' divorce and the unjust treatment of her professor. Her actions, when she was forced to stand alone, convinced them that Christ was real.

When Christians stand alone, the world has its best opportunity to see what Christ really means to them.

Reason #3: *Our teens will get into situations in which they have no one else to depend on except Christ.*

The prophet Jeremiah observed that our lives are radically changed when we stop depending on others and start depending on God.

> This is what the LORD says: "Cursed is the one who trusts in man, who depends on flesh for his strength and whose heart turns away from the LORD. He

will be like a bush in the wastelands. . . . He will
dwell in the parched places of the desert. . . . But
blessed is the man who trusts in the LORD, whose
confidence is in him. He will be like a tree planted
by the water that sends out its roots by the stream.
. . . It has no worries in a year of drought and never
fails to bear fruit" (Jeremiah 17:5–8).

In crisis situations, God helps our teen shift her dependence. As God leads her through one situation after another,
she learns to depend on Him because she has no other place to
go. Parents can anticipate this and teach teens not to fear the
times they will have to stand alone with Christ.

C.S. Lewis observed that we all tend to dread the situations God brings into our lives to force us to shift our center
of dependence.

It is a dreadful truth that the state of . . . "having to
depend solely on God" is what we all dread most.
And of course that just shows how very much,
how almost exclusively, we have been depending
on things . . . we will not turn to him as long as He
leaves us anything else to turn to. I suppose all one
can say is that it was bound to come. In the hour of
death and the day of judgment, what else shall we
have? Perhaps when those moments come, they
will feel happiest who have been forced . . . to
begin practising it here on earth. It is good of Him
to force us; but, dear me, how hard to feel that it is
good at the time.[*]

---

[*]C.S. Lewis, *Letters to an American Lady* (Grand Rapids:
Eerdmans, 1967), 49.

A perfectionist hits a dead end

Lincoln, a perfectionist, worked hard at controlling his world. He decided as a teenager that someday he would be a social worker so that he could make the world a better place. Then he chose the best Christian college he could find that had a major in this field of study.

As a freshman, he contacted a local Christian organization that he dreamed of working for someday. To his amazement and delight, they invited him to begin an internship with them.

At the church he attended, Lincoln publicly thanked the Lord for working everything out. "It's all to His glory," said Linc, with his life proceeding down the track he had carefully laid out, every event seemed right on schedule. Not for long, however.

Halfway into his first semester of college, Linc got some bad news. The organization he was interning for was moving so far away that he couldn't even afford to work for them during the summer.

Linc was angry. This messed up his plans.

Then, at the end of his freshman year, he received more bad news. *His college was closing down!* It would stay open one more year, so those who were about to become seniors could graduate. But at the end of Linc's sophomore year his college of choice would no longer exist.

Linc had to transfer to another college that had a strong social work major. However, at this non-Christian college the faculty and students were hostile toward everything Linc stood for.

Linc now felt completely abandoned by God. He struggled with why God would mess up all his plans. What was God up to?

Without this experience, Linc would have never learned to depend on God. For the first time in his life, Linc had to turn to the Lord to help him stand alone in a hostile environment.

Years later, Linc saw this period in his life as a strategic turning point. Without the experience of standing alone for Christ as a college student, Linc never would have developed the strength or vision to be a missionary to a hostile culture.

Strengthening our teen to stand alone with Christ means to equip her with a perspective that says, "It's good to be put in situations in which I have no one to trust except God. These situations, more than any other, make me into the kind of person God desires me to be."

The best little girl

Shauna, a senior in high school, had a preoccupation with food and body weight that became so serious she could no longer ignore it. A mixture of anorexic and bulimic behaviors were draining all her mental and physical energies and sabotaging all her other interests, goals, and relationships.

For a while, she didn't mind having this problem. It helped her feel superior to other people. Eventually, however, her eating disorders became a monster that ruled her life. She wanted to be free.

For help, she reached out to her parents, friends, teachers at school, and finally her pastor. With good intentions each of them gave her ideas and assignments to gain control over the problem. Although she earnestly tried every suggestion they gave her, nothing seemed to help.

At last, her parents took her to a Christian counselor. Wisely, the counselor helped Shauna trace her eating disorder to a deeply entrenched conviction that her life depended on convincing others that she was the "best little girl in the world."

Although Shauna believed in Christ and regarded him as her Savior, she depended on him very little for anything in life. Instead, she depended on what she could get from others by being a Christian Barbie doll.

The counselor recognized that God wanted to use Shauna's obsessions to shift her center of dependence. No one could help her overcome her problem except Christ. The counselor explained that without God's help, Shauna could never free herself from the conviction and resulting behaviors that held her captive.

At first, Shauna rejected this advice. Always able to figure out a way to get everything she had ever wanted, she wasn't ready to admit her helplessness. However, true to her counselor's words, the more Shauna tried to wrestle her problems into submission on her own, the more severe they became.

The breakthrough finally came one afternoon when Shauna arrived home from school.

No one else was home, and much to her dismay, someone had left two trays of freshly baked brownies on the counter. It was more than she could resist after going through the day denying herself anything to eat but sweetened hot water for breakfast, and a few celery sticks for lunch.

Shauna consumed every brownie on both trays in less than five minutes. Then, totally disgusted with herself, she raced to the bathroom and vomited. But the disgust didn't go away. She stared at herself in the mirror and felt total hopelessness. Shauna decided she would rather die than go on living this way.

For a moment the possibility of killing herself seemed so appealing that she became terrified she might actually do it. She turned and ran out of the house.

Still running ten minutes later, Shauna was out of breath. She slowed to a walk. Looking around, she realized she was on a hiking trail in a park about a mile from her home. *What am I going to do? I feel so alone,* she thought.

A verse from the Bible popped into her mind, "Draw near to God and He will draw near to you."

That reminded her of something her counselor had told her. "Until you stop acting like Barbie around God, and give Him a chance to love the real Shauna, your life will never change."

At that moment Shauna could only think of one thing that gave her any hope: Would God walk with her? Would He come to her now and be with her? It was the first time she could ever remember asking God just to be with her.

"God, I'm so ugly. I can't imagine why you'd want anything to do with me. But, please God, I need you. I have no one else to turn to but you. Will you walk with me in the park right now?"

That afternoon, Shauna experienced God's presence in her life for the first time. For two hours she felt bathed in His love. On the way home she found herself singing a tune she hadn't heard in years. "Turn your eyes upon Jesus. Look full in his wonderful face. And the things of earth will grow strangely dim in the light of his glory and grace."

Little did she realize the changes that were already starting to occur in her heart. The Barbie-doll identity her counselor helped her uncover was what started to grow strangely dim that afternoon. It began to lose its hold on Shauna as she chose to depend instead upon the grace and love of Christ.

Shauna's problem behaviors didn't disappear overnight. However, as she continued to walk with Christ in the same way she learned to walk with Him that afternoon in the park, she slowly shed her preoccupation with food and weight, like a child slowly loses interest in a pacifier or blanket.

God will guide all kids into stand-alone experiences because, ultimately, all of our teens will be separated from their parents and spiritual mentors. All of them will be deserted by their Christian friends. All of them will experience situations in which God is teaching them to depend on no one but himself.

Paul labored to strengthen Timothy for these experiences just as we should for our kids. Paul was very specific about the ways he wanted Timothy to stand on his own. He wrote, "For the time will come when men will not put up with sound doctrine. They will . . . turn aside to myths. But you, keep your head in all situations, endure hardship, do the work of an evangelist, discharge all the duties of your ministry" (2 Timothy 4:3–5).

What it means to stand alone with Christ

In these verses, Paul directed Timothy to handle pressure and opposition to his faith in four ways. By teaching our teens to follow these same practices, we strengthen them to stand alone.

Practice #1: *Don't panic—keep your head in all situations*

The worst thing a person can do in distress is panic. Lifeguards use the term *double drowning* to describe a situation in which the lifeguard who attempts to save a drowning person ends up drowning herself because the guard, also, loses her head and panics.

This is why the most important step in training lifeguards is to continue putting them in simulated rescue situations until they learn to keep their heads when things go wrong. Until a lifeguard learns to control her own panic impulses, she will remain a hazard to herself and other swimmers.

Ice diving

Scuba divers love diving under winter ice because everything is so quiet and clear. Aspen, a Wisconsin boy in his twenties, believed ice diving was the ultimate.

On one dive, however, Aspen and his buddy got separated under the water. Aspen's buddy was connected to a safety line, but somehow Aspen slipped off. Since it is almost impossible to find the hole in the ice without the line, you must obey a few basic rules when you lose the line: don't panic, stay where you are, conserve your air, and wait for your buddy to find you.

When Aspen lost the line, he had well over twenty minutes of air left. Only a few minutes passed before Aspen's buddy realized he was gone, and the buddy immediately followed the line back to the ice hole to get help. He and several others conducted a systematic search. In less than three minutes, they found Aspen—already dead—with a full fourteen minutes of air left in his tank!

Later, his cause of death was determined to be a heart attack suffered in a state of wild panic.

All of us must be strengthened to not panic during frightening and lonely periods in our lives. As our teenager enters adult years, she will be confronted with many circumstances like these. Without the kind of training lifeguards get, our teen could easily panic and make destructive decisions.

Paul's training for Timothy included sending him alone into hostile situations to serve Christ. On these short-term missions Timothy slowly developed the strength to stand alone.

We are wise to give our teen the same experiences. We should look for opportunities while she is still living with us, to send her alone into situations hostile to her faith—whether it's a school, job, or community setting.

There, her loyalty to Christ will be tested. It will be exposed as weak, or it will be made stronger. Either way, we'll be nearby to rescue her if necessary and help her grow from the experience.

Practice #2: *Don't give up—endure hardship*

Most of the time, living the Christian life isn't a team sport. Most of what God calls us to do for Him must be done when other Christians are not around to keep us motivated or energized.

Paul challenged Timothy to keep going even when no one was there to cheer him on. He often asked Timothy to serve Christ in ways that were difficult, grueling, and private so that Timothy wouldn't depend on the applause of anyone except God.

Church youth ministries often offer superb experiences for Christian growth and service to our teens. However, the danger is that our teen could grow to depend too much on her youth programs and leaders and do little on her own to serve Christ. This weakens the spiritual muscles she'll need someday to stand alone.

We must encourage our teen to participate in some solo enterprises for Christ that are unassisted, uncelebrated, uncompensated, long-term, and behind the scenes. Such enterprises should force her to be apart from her friends for a while and experience what it means to be a private servant for Christ.

Activities could include babysitting for a needy mother, caring for an aging neighbor, volunteering as a manual laborer for a Christian organization, or writing letters to missionaries. There are hundreds of other possibilities.

When we encourage teenagers to participate in these kinds of endeavors, we strengthen them for the day God will call them to stand alone.

Practice #3: *Don't shut up—do the work of an evangelist*

Paul knew that standing alone with Christ many times meant standing up for Him. When we're standing alone we may try to survive by blending in, calling no attention to ourselves. But, Paul strengthened Timothy to take a noisy stand for Christ.

When God asked Moses to take a stand for Him against the pharaoh of Egypt, Moses refused because he wasn't good at speaking persuasively about his faith. "O, Lord, I have never been eloquent, neither in the past nor since you have spoken to your servant. I am slow of speech and tongue" (Exodus 4:10).

Just like Moses, someday our teenager may hesitate to stand alone for Christ if she doesn't know what to say.

We strengthen teenagers to stand alone when we train them to speak evangelistically with others about their faith. There's no better way to do this, than to follow a simple three-step plan.

1. Let them watch us do it first (perhaps a talk with a neighbor or a cultist who comes to our door)
2. Teach them how we did it (giving them a basic outline or tool, such as The Four Spiritual Laws booklet)
3. Let them do it while we watch (in a children's Bible school class or on a missions trip).

Even though our teen may not turn around and use this training to take a stand for Christ in junior high or high school, she'll be more prone to do it as an adult because we showed her how to do the work of an evangelist—something God calls every Christian to do.

Practice #4: *Don't get unbalanced—discharge all the duties of your ministry*

Under pressure, feeling all alone, it's easy to become unbalanced. We shift into a crisis mode and focus solely on the problem at hand, forgetting the daily routines and disciplines that keep us healthy and strong.

Paul knew Timothy had a tendency to neglect critical areas of his life (health, relationships, prayer life) when he was standing alone under pressure. This played right into the hands of Timothy's spiritual enemies. By drawing him into a prolonged debate or controversy, the enemies got him to neglect the very responsibilities that made him dangerous to them. They ultimately weakened his stand by so preoccupying him with a single issue that it created an imbalance in his life.

When we become unbalanced, we lose our spiritual perspective and vitality and our ability to stand by ourselves.

For this reason, Paul always encouraged balance in Timothy's life and ministry. Warning Timothy not to get absorbed in controversies, Paul urged him to spend time in a variety of tasks with a variety of people, balancing his time between enriching his own spiritual life and enriching others.

Encouraging balance is one of the best ways we can prepare teenagers to go the distance without us.

In a way, we are erecting guardrails along the highway of life. Whenever we see our teen straying too far to the right or left (by focusing too much or too little on a particular area of her life), we can act as a guardrail and call her back to center.

We also help our kids when we challenge false dichotomies they set up, making some things spiritual and some things not. Sometimes, our teen might choose to neglect her health, her studies, even her family because she doesn't consider these duties spiritual enough to warrant her time and energy.

Paul made it clear to Timothy that everything we do as Christians is a ministry in the name of Christ. Even mundane or routine tasks that we do to take care of ourselves or others are spiritual activities. Keeping this perspective helps us maintain balance in life.

Learning to keep their balance in times of stress will strengthen our teenagers to stand alone.

The most important thing parents can do

Although Paul did many things to strengthen Timothy, he knew Timothy's stance would be only as strong as the ground he was standing on. The strongest athlete in the world has trouble staying on his feet without solid footing.

Even today's marketing specialists know that their ability to perpetuate consumer loyalty is only as strong as the products or services they provide. Loyalty stays strong when it is resting on something solid.

This is why Paul never encouraged Timothy to give his loyalty to a goal, cause, organization, or Christian leader. None of these would be solid enough to generate loyalty that lasts a lifetime. The only ground solid enough to keep Timothy standing was a deeply held affection for Jesus Christ. Paul said, "You then, my son, be strong in the grace that is in Christ Jesus" (2 Timothy 2:1).

Strengthening Timothy's affection for Jesus Christ was the single most important thing Paul ever did for his son in the faith.

Paul spoke of Christ often. He longed to be with Jesus more than anyone. He constantly told Timothy stories about his own personal experiences with Christ. Paul wrote, "Even though I was once a blasphemer and a persecutor and a violent man, I was shown mercy. . . . The grace of our Lord was poured out on me abundantly, along with the faith and love that are in Christ Jesus" (1 Timothy 1:13–14).

Paul showed Timothy, by the risks he took and the suffering he endured, that Christ's love for him was always solid. When kids see this kind of affection for Jesus Christ in their parents, it leaves an indelible impression.

Memories from the mountains

Joshua was born in Appalachian country and remembers his father's infectious love for Christ. This is how he tells his story:

Everything about Jesus Christ and the Bible was exciting to my father. He would tell us stories from the Bible as if they were from books that had won a Pulitzer prize. He got excited about the disciple Philip being zapped through space into the desert. He'd always cry when telling us about Jesus dying on the cross. He'd read the Psalms as if they were Shakespeare. He'd memorize passages and then recite them to us.

He'd get up in the morning and thank God for the sunshine. He'd even thank God for the snow—although it made it difficult to get around the mountains.

He'd watch the birds and shake his head in awe of what God had made. He'd look at his beloved mountains and congratulate God for their beauty.

But the most exciting thing to him was the wonderful opportunities he had to serve people. He felt that God had put him down here on earth to show the same love for people that Jesus Christ had.

My father had a quiet confidence about God's mission for him. No one could shake it. He did some teaching back up in the "branches" and "hollows" of the mountains. His teaching incorporated all subjects—but God was always at the heart of all material.

That bothered some of the people, and one day while he was teaching me and a bunch of the other kids in our one-room schoolhouse, shots rang out and bullets thudded into the ground just outside the door. Three men who didn't want any of my father's teachings in their neck of the woods were firing at him.

"Caleb!" they yelled. "We want you to get out of here and stay out. We don't want any of your kind of learning."

We recognized the voice and knew the danger was real. However, my father said not to pay any attention. "We've got the story of how God led the Israelites through the wilderness to discuss right now," he said.

The class went ahead, but a few minutes later, shots rang out again.

"What's the matter, Caleb?" came the same chilling voice. "Are you scared . . . afraid to come out?"

My father never responded. He went on to talk about how God fed His people in the desert with manna. But we all wondered what would happen after the lesson was over.

The shouting continued, and when my father finally finished the Bible lesson, he announced, "OK, boys and girls. It's recess time!"

My father went out with us, just like he always did. When we started to play ball, he volunteered to pitch, knowing it made him an easy target for a sharpshooter.

Recess came and went. We went back into the schoolhouse and finished the day as if nothing had happened, and the men never bothered us at school again.

Eventually, those same men became Christians through my father's teachings, and years later, one of them told me, "We had him in our sights, but we couldn't pull the trigger. Something wouldn't let us. I know it was God!"

Joshua never forgot his dad's standing alone for Christ that day on the ball field. Just recalling the memory strengthened him to do the same any time he had the opportunity.

As parents, we have no idea what is in store for our teen-agers—how or when God will ask them to stand alone for Him. Nevertheless, all through their lives, we should be strengthening them for that day.

The best way we can do that is to help our teen fall in love with Jesus Christ.

It's the only foundation for a faith that lasts.

Study Guide

There are three principles to remember as we study this book.

Principle #1: *This book has a "we" feel to it.*

Guiding Your Teen to a Faith That Lasts is written horizontally—as if we were all sitting together in a room, sharing with each other as good friends. This book should not be studied as a vertical book, where the authors, the group leaders, or some other "expert" is preaching down to the other members of the group.

Principle #2: *Encourage everyone to take part.*

Everybody in the group has something to offer. No one has an edge on guiding teens to faith that lasts, so do all you can to assure that everybody has a chance to contribute to the discussion.

Principle #3: *Consider the "extra credit" sections.*

Your group can decide to have everyone work on these sections each week and report back as one group, or the group could divide into smaller groups, with a different small group assigned to do the "extra credit" work each time you meet. Use the approach that will insure the most participation.

Chapter 1: *Why Are We Losing Our Kids?*

1. What is the question every teen must be allowed to ask?

2. In what ways could we be guilty of the same lack of love exhibited by Rob's youth pastor?

3. What is our greatest task as Christian parents?

4. In 1 Thessalonians 3:5, Paul expressed the common fear we parents have. How does this fear affect the way we parent?

5. In one sentence describe the message your life is most likely sending your teen.

Extra Credit

The Passion Meter

1. The thing I was most passionate about this week (so passionate my teen could see it) was _____.

2. The thing I was most passionate about this year was
_____.

3. What does this passion teach my teen about life?
_____
_____
_____.

Chapter 2: *Why Our Teen's Faith Doesn't Last*

1. Describe five kinds of drifters. Do any of them describe what we were like as teenagers?

2. Paul identified Cephas as what kind of drifter in 2 Timothy 4:9–10?

3. Which kind of drifter is the hardest for each of us to spot? To deal with? Why?

4. How can we spot dominators like Jo-Lynn and Matt?

5. What can we do specifically to help each kind of drifting teenager?

Extra Credit

News Flash!

Using newspaper, magazine, radio, movie, or TV, come up with an example of each of the five kinds of drifters.

Deserter _____.

Disputer _____.

Deceiver _____.

Dominator _____.

Defeated _____.

Chapter 3: *How the Enemy Calls Our Teen*
Away From the Faith

1. What is Satan's objective with our teen as indicated by Paul in 2 Timothy 2:26?

2. Describe the different traps Satan uses to intoxicate our teen.

3. What three signs indicate our teen is trapped?

4. What is the R.E.S.T. strategy?

     R _____

     E _____

     S _____

     T _____

Extra Credit

Journal Time
This week, I saw my teen rebel by . . . _____ _____ _____
I was able to use the R.E.S.T. strategy in the following way . . . _____ _____ _____
The result was . . . _____ _____

Chapter 4: *How Faith Takes Hold and Grows In Our Teen*

1. What is our teen's question (and our answer) at each of the "Seven Stages of Faith Building"?

HEARING
Question:_____ Our answer: _____

FLIRTING
Question:_____ Our answer: _____

STUDYING
Question:_____ Our answer: _____

TESTING
Question:_____ Our answer: _____

EMBRACING
Question:_____ Our answer: _____

SPREADING
Question:_____ Our answer: _____

SUFFERING
Question:_____ Our answer: _____

Extra Credit

When It Happened To Me		
Hearing Age:____	Situation:_____	Result:_____
Flirting Age:____	Situation:_____	Result:_____
Studying Age:____	Situation:_____	Result:_____
Testing Age:____	Situation:_____	Result:_____
Embracing Age:____	Situation:_____	Result:_____
Spreading Age:____	Situation:_____	Result:_____
Suffering Age:____	Situation:_____	Result:_____

Chapter 5: *Faith-Building Skills Our Teen Must Learn*

1. Describe each of the faith-building skills Paul described in 2 Timothy 2.

2. Tell how we learned a faith-building skill growing up. How did our parents help?

3. Which of these skills is the most important in our minds?

4. What lesson did Hank's peanut butter jar example teach Gary?

5. Are there other faith-building skills that we could add to this list of six?

Extra Credit

Choose a Skill	
When I was a kid . . . (tell how I learned one of the faith-building skills)	Now that I'm a parent . . . (tell how I'm going to attempt to teach my teen a skill)

Chapter 6: *Exposing Our Teen to the Contagious Lives of Passionate Christians*

1. Why is it better for our teen to see us "transfigured" instead of perfect?

2. Describe a time you were spiritually helped by a little incarnation, transfiguration, crucifixion, or resurrection *in another person's life.*

3. Describe a time when you experienced a little incarnation, transfiguration, crucifixion, or resurrection *in your own life.* How did it affect your child?

4. How did God use the tragic circumstances facing Scott's mom to teach a powerful lesson?

5. Are we *really* ready to experience "little transfigurations" in our life? What will be the consequences?

Extra Credit

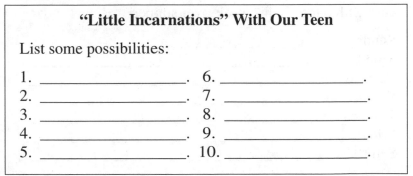

"Little Incarnations" With Our Teen

List some possibilities:

1. _____.   6. _____.
2. _____.   7. _____.
3. _____.   8. _____.
4. _____.   9. _____.
5. _____.   10. _____.

Chapter 7: *Inoculating Our Teen Against the Enemies of Christ*

1. How can we inoculate our teen in a spiritual sense?

2. What does Barry's experience teach us about "hating non-Christians"?

3. What makes inoculation so hard for us as Christian parents?

4. What four tasks does inoculation involve?

    a. _____

    b. _____

    c. _____

    d. _____

5. How will it be helpful to our teen if our church is reaching out to our community?

Extra Credit

What Did We "Have" for Supper?

Meals are a wonderful time to talk about the enemies of Christ with our teens. List possible topics that we could discuss with our teen this week over supper.

Sunday _____

Monday _____

Tuesday _____

Wednesday _____

Thursday _____

Friday _____

Saturday _____

Chapter 8: *Inviting Our Teen on a Mission for Christ*

1. What three elements characterized Paul's "mission trips for Christ"?

2. Why is the "Matthew 6:33 principle" so important to a mission trip for Christ?

3. What are the five pitfalls to avoid on missions trips?

4. Talk about the kind of mission trip we'd like to design for our family.

5. What is meant by the phrase "the unexpected is often the most remembered" . . . especially as it applies to the Dakota trip?

Extra Credit

Trip Evaluation

1. List a mission trip for Christ that our family took.
2. Did it meet Paul's three-point criteria?
3. Did it expose the hearts of our family?
4. Did it reveal who Christ is?
5. Did it capture our teen's imagination?
6. Did it avoid the "five pitfalls"?
7. Did something unexpected happen that revealed God in a new way?
8. Do we have any more planned for the future?

Chapter 9: *Teaching Our Teen How to Use the Bible*

1. What wrong conclusion do teens sometimes have about the Bible?

2. What is so unusual about the origin of the Bible?

3. How can we help our teen experience the Bible as Paul described it in 2 Timothy 3:16–17?

4. Explain the "Corrupt Government in . . . Our Hearts."

Extra Credit

Book Report Time

Find three great historical figures and report back on the importance of the Bible in their daily lives—or at pivotal points in their lives. Some examples:

Christopher Columbus, Abraham Lincoln, Robert E. Lee, Stonewall Jackson, Isaac Newton, Susanna Wesley, Samuel Morse, George Washington Carver.